P9-BHW-345

# New England Town Affairs

# New England Town Affairs

by
An Indigent Participant
Charles J. Lincoln, Esq.
Town Counsel

Illustrations by Jack Zwalley

Covered Bridge Press
North Attleboro, Massachusetts

Copyright © 1995, by Covered Bridge Press.
All rights reserved.

No part of this book may be reproduced in any form without the
express written permission of the publisher.

Covered Bridge Press
7 Adamsdale Road
N. Attleboro, MA 02761

Second Printing

# Contents

# Exculpatory Foreword

Most books of any consequence begin with a foreword by some obscure scholar, who has been enticed into lending his name to the effort in order to give it some class, or as is more likely to be the case, in order for the author to have someone with whom to share the blame in case it bombs.

A good foreword has another purpose; it just might reveal the thrust of the work, especially if it isn't too clear from the text what it is all about. This assumes that the writer of the foreword has in fact read the text, and knows, or thinks he knows, what it is saying. It is right here that this foreword falls apart at the seams.

To begin with, I haven't read the text and have no intention of ever doing so, having spent a number of fruitless years taking a reading on the author himself. This has led me to the inescapable conclusion that any further association with either of them might be an admission against interest—mine.

Furthermore, nobody in his right mind would admit to being an authority on, let alone attempt to explain away, all the devious little schemes that have occupied the attention of the author over the years, one of them being this book.

About the best that can be said of a project of this sort, without fear of reprisals, is that history has taught us that whenever things get bad enough, some fool with more gall than brains always seems to bubble up through the silt of life and write a book about it. These blindingly lucid exposés point the finger of truth and

1

light right at the heart of the problem, something the author thinks we lesser mortals are incapable of doing for ourselves.

In its highest form, this sort of carrying-on occasionally produces martyrs. In its lowest form, it accounts for an endless trickle of letters to the editor on a variety of inconsequential matters.

Somewhere in between can be found the excuse for a book like this one.

To the extent that what follows needs a foreword, let the foregoing be it.


William L. Edwards, Esq.
Moved; left no forwarding address

# Introduction
# and Disclaimer

Some people just can't leave well enough alone; they have to write a book about it, as though that can purge their souls. That's the only explanation I can think of for this effort.

I believe I am correct in this notion, because as a former First Selectman of our town, where the events described further along took place, I have personal knowledge of the author's involvement in many of them. To suggest that he viewed them in an unconventional light is a gross understatement. I must say, however, in the interest of historical accuracy, that while the main thrust is substantially correct, the author appears to have taken certain liberties with some of the details.

For just one example, in the chapter dealing with the town dump and its successor, the sanitary landfill, he implies, very cavalierly, that the thing cost about four hundred grand to launch. Well, he's way off base; the last time I knew anything about it, the actual cost was more like a million nine, and still climbing.

I cannot attest to the accuracy of the section recounting the perambulation of town bounds, because during my tenure as a selectman, I studiously avoided the whole thing. A man of my age could be writing this posthumously if he even thought of stumbling around in the woods and swamps performing that ritual.

Unfortunately, the section on town meetings is also somewhat out of date. At the last Town Meeting I presided over, the Moderator insisted on voting on the recommendations of the

Ways and Means Committee, rather than on the warrant article itself, which always promoted some malcontent to insist on a vote by checklist and ballot, causing an awful problem.

As the town grew, and the number of people attending Town Meeting increased dramatically, a subtle change occurred; there seemed to be more people attending the meeting than were entitled to vote. It was obvious that there were some ringers in the crowd when the checklist and ballot routine revealed that less than half the people in the hall were legal voters.

We thought we had the problem licked when a new resident of town, an electrical engineer, devised a scheme for issuing every registered voter a Registered Voter Card—a little, plastic thing that could be inserted into a reader at the door, just like when you go through the checkout line at the supermarket. If the reader showed a green light, the holder was admitted.

It seemed foolproof, except that Visa and Master Cards would also work in the reader. Paid-up credit cards would show green, while cards in arrears would show red. A lot of upstanding citizens were denied admission to the town hall for the wrong reasons. The electrical engineer is trying to figure out how to solve this additonal little problem at this very minute.

Life in the puckerbrush has its share of problems too.

Cyrus "Cy" Tuttle
Former First Selectman
Now of Sun City, Florida

# Qualified Endorsement by the Citizens' Committee for a Better Amherst

For nearly two hundred years New Hampshirites have been pounding away at such things as the Free Silver Movement, the New Deal, the Fair Deal, and more recently the Great Society, with varying degrees of success. The Society of Colonial Dames haven't quite put the lid on the United Empire Loyalists, but since the very last Loyalist in town is pushing 94, nobody will mind our revealing the peculiarities of the institutions that make this sort of carrying-on possible. This is especially pertinent today, because the rest of the world is so obviously hanging around waiting for something to straighten it out, when all the time we've had the secret.

It s not that our townsfolk are a particularly reactionary group, bent on resisting change. They recognize that where they have been unable to thwart it, change is inevitable. Zoning is an example: a vocal element among the old-timers were able to resist this invasion of their right to do whatever they damn-well please with their property for only ten or twelve years.

Nor have we had any problem accommodating to the strictures of the civil rights movement, because none of them live here; they can't afford to.

That leaves the Women's Movement, but that hasn't been a problem either. The women around town have been fully engaged propagating and running the PTA, which serves as an outlet for whatever spare energy they have left. The ones that have survived their child-bearing years wind up joining the King's Daughters, and they're not a particularly militant group at the moment.

Even the Boston Globe Cane, traditionally passed on to the oldest resident of town, hasn't changed hands for the past eleven years. However, this may change momentarily. The present holder of the cane slipped on one of his grandchildren's roller skates, and is said not to be doing too well.

In short, about the only way to discover how it all really works is to read this book, a microscopic portion of the proceeds of which—assuming there are any—will be devoted to the work of the Committee for a Better Amherst.

COMMITTEE FOR A BETTER AMHERST
Percy Timbrell, Col. USA (Retired)
Chairman (Deceased)

# Judicial Caveat

Anyone who elects to live in a small town for more than a year inevitably gets caught up in the affairs and doings of the community one way or another. It is not possible to live in such a community without getting involved, voluntarily or otherwise.

A few people go overboard in this involvement business once they get the hang of it, and throwing caution to the winds, find themselves on all sorts of committees, participating in groups studying this or that, and, in terminal cases, running for public office. Even those who don't aspire to such lofty heights get drafted to fill appointive positions, especially if they make their living at some trade or profession remotely (at best) connected with the appointive office.

The local druggist became the health officer, whose main duty was approving the design of new septic systems about town. A fellow who worked for an electronic firm down in Nashua became chairman of The Committee on Computer Applications, the sole purpose of which was to persuade the town treasurer, a lady of many moons, to bring her office into the twentieth century by introducing computerized bookkeeping. This was deemed a real necessity because she was already two years behind with her pen and pencil routines; she had the town checkbook balanced, but she had no idea where all the money went.

It was my fate to be drafted as justice of the local Municipal Court, a position that paid a pittance—but think of all the prestige! However, the role of justice did have certain advantages, in that it isolated me from direct participation in any other of the town's routine workings.

"Never can tell when this issue may wind up in court," I would intone, enabling me to escape arduous duty on the Committee to Select an Architect for the New School.

I was also Town Counsel, a position that occasionally paid actual money, but that involved me only in the Grand Causes the Selectmen brought to my attention. As Judge and Town Counsel, I was in a fine position to gaze down upon the routine tugging and hauling of the citizenry as they went about their daily activities without actually getting my feet wet—clammy maybe, but not wet.

Within these pages are memorialized some of the weighty matters that came to my attention over some 27 years of washing in and out with the legal tides of town affairs. None of the events herein recalled are truly earth-shaking, and history would not be the loser if they never came to light at all, but like the chocolate sauce on the vanilla ice cream, they add a certain something to the dish.

Charles J. Lincoln, Esq.,
Professional Indigent

# Town Water

In this day and age when some of our most basic services are piped right into our houses, few of us give much thought to where they come from or where they eventually go when we're through with them. Water and sewer service are obvious examples. In the puckerbrush, water generally comes from wells, and when people are through with it, it winds up in the septic tank along with whatever else they may ingest. To that extent, both of these devices can be said to deal with renewable resources. Unfortunately, the proximity of these two devices to each other can be a problem for those who have not developed an immunity to that most pervasive of ailments, the green apple two-step. This doesn't bother the locals, who over the years have developed the necessary immunity, but for the newcomers, it can be devastating. At least this is the generally accepted version of what eventually overtook our town back in the 1980s.

Amherst was, and to some extent remains, a classic New England country town, complete with white clapboard houses, a village green, a carriage road, a Congregational Church (the Baptists operate out of a converted barn just outside the town center), a country store, a firehouse, and a town hall—all of which have been faithfully preserved through historical accident. The hurricane of 1938 ended rail service, and the main highway running through town was moved to higher ground, but other than that, the place hasn't changed much in the past 200 years. In fact these very qualities relegated the town to backwater status until the early 1960s, when its authentic and tranquil ambiance began to attract the forerunners of the Yuppies, the Gray-Flannel-Suiters, who flocked into the state to power the growing electronics industry that began to bloom in nearby Manchester and Nashua. These types, with money to burn, began to buy up the classic old houses around town which were being sold by the Old Timers, bent on cashing in at prices that made their heads spin. There are those who said that two of the stately old houses around the village green sold for more than the whole town cost initially. Then trouble began to brew.

Ever since the very first settler settled, everyone relied on wells for their drinking water, and privies to get rid of it when they were done with it, until the introduction of the septic tank, which took everything. The arrival of this contrivance had major appeal, since it enabled people to install flushing facilities right inside their houses, thereby eliminating the need to tramp through the winter snow to answer the call of nature. The problem with this new device was that while it took everything, it required great quantities of water to do its thing, all of which eventually wound up in the back yard, where it made its way back to the well. The traditional privy used a piling-up process, whereas the septic tank used a dispersal process, whereby the well was constantly replenished by the overflow from the septic system, giving rise to epidemics of the two-step, until an immunity had been built up against it.

It didn't take the newcomers long to discover that the source of their recurring intestinal upheavals was the network of adjacent, and sometimes interconnecting, wells and septic systems. One or the other of them had to go if digestive peace was to be restored. The Gray-Flannel-Suiters didn't have time to develop an evolutionary immunity in a situation where Kaopectate was only a temporary solution.

The Gray-Flannel-Suiters, grabbing the bull by the horns, offered an article at the next town meeting authorizing the establishment of a Village Water Precinct, for the express purpose of installing a town water system, but the article didn't pass.

The Old Timers just couldn't see the need for such an expenditure, when they had lived in town for generations without difficulty. As one of them observed, "You newcomers are just not as tough as we are. Anyway, what was good enough for my ancestors is good enough for me, and if was good enough for them, it's good enough for you, too."

A Committee of the Whole was then appointed to look into the matter, to which the Old Timers didn't offer much opposition, because they knew full well that Committees of the Whole have everlasting life, and seldom come up with anything before the issue they are charged with examining is supplanted by some other more pressing matter. But being wary, they made sure they were liberally represented on the committee.

There are no existing minutes of any deliberations of the committee. The few people still around from the time say the Gray-Flannel-Suiters pointed out that it was they who had paid the outlandish home prices demanded by the Old Timers, that this practice clearly added to the value of property all over town—including those still owned by the Old Timers—and that if they seriously opposed the new water system, they would be biting the hand that fed them. Furthermore, the water system would not extend to the entire town, but only the central portion of it where the Gray-Flannel-Suiters lived, and which alone would carry the added taxes caused by the installation of the system.

This crafty argument struck a responsive chord with the Old Timers. If it wasn't going to cost them anything because most of them lived outside the central part of the town, then let the newcomers have their newfangled water system.

"Cain't do us no harm," they said.

Thus it came to pass that at the next annual town meeting, the article authorizing the new water system, and the bonds to pay for it, was adopted. The years rolled along, the incidence of green apple two-step declined, and after twenty years, the bonds were retired and the system fully paid for. What did escape everyone's notice was that the Water Precinct was still collecting revenue, which about the time the firemen wanted a new fire truck, was ample for the purpose.

Over the years, the Old Timers were supplanted by their children, who became the New Old Timers, and the Gray-Flannel-Suiters became the Yuppies of today. The issue however, remains the same—what to do with the continuing flow of revenue from the water system?

The Yuppies wanted it to be devoted to "improving our schools," which the fruits of their recreational activities had overcrowded.

The New Old Timers wanted to use it to pave the dirt roads by their properties. The firemen wanted it used to purchase a new pumper. Everyone it seemed, had an urgent need.

The issue was joined at the next town meeting, when an article appeared in the warrant, authorizing the purchase of a new pumper, the balance, less down payment, to be raised by the town. Arguments ran hot and heavy, with the Yuppies taking an analytical approach, which the firemen didn't understand, therefore suspecting it was probably Communist-inspired.

As is the case in small towns throughout New England, nobody in his right mind ever votes against the firemen. To do so is to invite disaster, because if they get the slightest inkling that they are not appreciated, being volunteers, they'll all resign *en masse* for a week or so, and if anyone lets his cookout get away from him, he'll just have to stomp out the blaze with his feet.

When the matter came up for a vote, the Moderator appointed the fire chief and his deputy to count the show of hands, for and against. Just before the vote, the fire chief was heard to say to his deputy, "You count the no votes on your side of the hall, and I'll count them on my side, and then let's hope none of them ever has a fire." That did the trick; the article passed without a single dissenting vote.

But the problem was not solved. The Water Precinct still had to approve devoting some of its funds to the down payment, which called for a vote of the residents of the Water Precinct, most of whom were Yuppies.

Being crafty types, the Yuppies knew that regardless of the vote at Town Meeting, the real vote would occur at the Water Precinct meeting, because the Water Precinct controlled the funds the firemen needed for the down payment on the new fire truck. The Yuppies figured they had this one in the bag regardless of how the vote turned out in the Town Meeting.

Over the years, the Water Precinct meetings had deteriorated into lackluster affairs. In the last few years the meetings seldom had a quorum present, a fact the Yuppies figured would prevent a valid vote on any appropriation of funds. All they had to do was boycott the meeting, and they'd have it aced, they thought. However, they did not fully appreciate the tactical abilities of the local firemen.

The firemen perceived what was at stake, and showed up unannounced, in force. The Yuppies, thinking the thing was dead anyway without them, failed to turn out at all. An unconfirmed report has it that the firemen contrived to have the precinct meeting held on the same night as the PTA meeting, and the Yuppies, being big in that terribly important group, turned out in force in support of whatever that organization promoted. About the only people attending the Water Precinct meeting were the firemen, who, seeing victory within their grasp, locked the doors and immediately put the matter of the down payment to a vote. Naturally, it was carried.

Flushed with victory, the firemen proceeded to move the question, amend, and amend the amendment, before closing with a motion to flush the entire water system with applejack, cut off service to the parsonage, and hold next year's meeting in Monaco.

The net result of all these parliamentary moves was that the firemen got their $3,400 for the down payment in the new fire truck, which, when added to the sum appropriated at Town Meeting, guaranteed the purchase of the new pumper.

What records exist of the doings of the Water Precinct meeting are blurred with what appear to be coffee stains. However, a sufficient number of Old Timers still exist to confirm the foregoing history, should anyone be so injudicious as to question this account.

Most of the Yuppies have left town.

# The Town
# Clock Caper

Most New England towns have a few historical fixtures dating back to the eighteenth century, and Amherst is among them. In addition to the traditional Congregational Church, complete with tall steeple and spire, it boasts a set of Paul Revere bells, which are the property of the church. It also contains the town clock, which is the property of the town, a municipal corporation, said to be without religious affiliation.

Until fairly recently, the issue of separation of church and state, brought about by this arrangement of bric-à-brac, hadn't reared its ugly head. The Sexton of Cemeteries would toll the bells every Sunday by gently pulling the bell rope that hung down in the vestibule of the church. He insisted on personally performing this task because his additional duties required him to keep the town clock running with its usual carefree abandon. Excessive tolling of the bells tended to upset the escapement of the clock, which caused it to perform with a certain indifference until he could climb up into into the steeple and give it a kick—something he found difficult to do after he passed his eightieth birthday.

In order to avoid random tolling of the bells, the Sexton adopted the practice of unhooking the bell rope on December 31st each year to thwart New Year's revelers, who were addicted to the time-honored tradition of vigorously tolling the bells at the stroke of midnight on New Year's Eve. Electronic engineers and insurance agents, among some of the newer residents of town, found this activity particularly gratifying.

The entire problem involving the clock arose a few years ago when some revelers, finding the bell rope missing, elected to scale the steeple in search of the rope. They climbed up through the works of the clock and into the belfry, and began to toll the bells by bracing themselves against the weather boards, and vigorously kicking the bells with their feet to get them swinging. This was going along fairly well until one reveler, bracing himself against the weather boards, gave a particularly hard kick. The weather boards gave way, and he found himself dangling, half in the belfry and half out, with nothing between him and the ground but about 90 feet of cool night air.

Naturally, this turn of events had a sobering effect. Everyone climbed down from the belfry and immediately summoned the church Elders to advise these worthies of the lamentable state of repair of their steeple and the belfry. Unfortunately there are no minutes of the doings of this meeting, other than that it was held at 1:30 in the morning and lasted all of five minutes, just long enough to appoint a committee to look into the matter and report back.

After extensive research, the committee rendered its preliminary report, in which it ascertained that, working from the ground up (a) the church owned the church, (b) the town owned the clock and related works and structures, and (c) the church owned the bells and belfry. Above the belfry the church had undertaken to erect a still taller structure, a steeple, that towered another 50 feet or so toward Heaven. Thus the clock, being midway up this pile of timbers, clapboards and fretwork, supported one of the finest examples of what a proper belfry and steeple should look like. All this was in grave danger of collapse, the report stated, due to the ravages of old age, termites, fungus, or some other form of non-Christian dry rot, to mention only a few of the possibilities. It required immediate repair, the report said, if the whole thing was not to come crashing down.

To be sure of their ground, the Elders commissioned an engineering report to ascertain the full extent of the problem. Proposals were solicited on how to fix it, and what the fix might cost. The result staggered the Elders. The lowest bid called for an expenditure of some $14,000, just to make sure the whole thing didn't collapse into the church vestibule. What really shocked everyone was that this figure was after the clergyman's discount.

For a while it was rumored that the bid was obviously inspired by the Catholics, but this was put to rest when it was revealed that the bid was submitted by a member of the choir, who was also in the building business. Obviously some means had to be found to spread out the load, assuming the figure was correct.

Some thought was given to a public appeal but calmer heads prevailed, pointing out that the separation of church and state must be considered. There were apt to be a few Baptists, Episcopalians and Methodists along with some other less well-defined persuasions who might object to a public appeal on behalf of a partisan group, especially if it was done under the guise of a town project. In order to resolve this impasse, a Committee of the Whole was convened, which came up with a solution with the speed of light, belying their collective ages. Their reasoning ran something like this: (a) on the bottom is the church; (b) halfway up is the town clock, which is public (town) property; (c) above that is the belfry and the steeple, which is church property; (d) if the belfry is weakened by termites, they didn't just jump up there; they gnawed their way up through the town clock, and if the town had properly attended to its maintenance over the years, the termites would have been detected before they had a chance of eating away the supports for the church s belfry and steeple.

It was therefore only a small step to suggest that town negligence had impaired the integrity of the church's belfry and steeple, making the town responsible for the repairs. A letter in furtherance of this conclusion, along with a demand for $17,000 in damages, was sent to the Selectmen. The Elders figured a small margin was necessary in their demand in order to give them some bargaining room.

For a while the Selectmen thought they had the Elders where the hair is short because they appeared to have overlooked a simple but critical consideration. To get to the town clock, the termites had to first chew up through the church itself.

"If you fellows claim your belfry is in danger because of our termites, well, how the hell do you figure those termites managed to get into our clock supports without first making their way up there, right through your church?" the chairman of the Board of Selectmen demanded. "If you can come up with a plausible answer to that one, maybe we can work something out. Until then, you fellows had better set about repairing your church before we have to bill you for the destruction of our clock," he concluded.

To lesser men, this might have been their undoing, but not for the Elders. They hadn't been around as long as they had without picking up a few defensive tactics.

"Now don't you boys get all het up just yet," they said. "Have you fellows read your lease?" asked the eldest Elder.

Lease? What lease? Nobody ever heard of any lease, especially one with regard to the town clock. The eldest Elder then carefully spread out before the Selectmen an old, musty, yellowed document, written in fine Victorian handwriting, and called their attention to the fourth paragraph, which as nearly as anyone could tell, read as follows:

*The Society shall provide a suitable place for the installation of the towne clock, the repair and maintenance of which shall be the responsibility of the Shire, and for the privilege of displaying which the Shire shall pay the Society the sum of One Dollar each and every year hereafter, or until the Lord calleth us all.*

Now here was a bind. When was the last time the Shire—now the town—paid the rent? If the town was in default on the rent, did it have a leg to stand on? Could it be evicted, forcing it to remove the town clock? The town records would have to be consulted, and this was no mean task.

Two months later the best educated guess was that the last recorded payment had been made in 1882. The arrears, together the statutory interest, which the Elders were sure to claim, represented a sum the Selectmen could hardly charge to their over-and-short account without a vote of the entire town.

Not only that, the eldest Elder raised the specter of the town being evicted from the church, requiring it to remove the town clock. At best, the town could be charged as a mere trespasser and at worst, it might incur tremendous liability if by chance the clock, bells and steeple all came crashing down, wiping out the pulpit some Sunday morning.

But not to be outdone by the Elders, the Selectmen countered with the observation that "Maybe you people don't own the church at all. Where is your deed? Without that you have no standing and we can't even negotiate with you."

Surely, if they could find that old lease, the Elders could come up with the deed to the church—somehow. The stage was set, and the battle joined. The Selectmen enlisted the aid of Town Counsel, instructing him to "See what you can come up with. We can't let a matter of this magnitude die a natural death. Might even get the Grange in the picture; they're apt to be a lively group, you know."

At Town Counsel's salary, there wasn't much room for anything but languid research, not that is, until winter set in, and there was time to pore over the old town records. While engaged in this activity, Town Counsel became aware that someone had preceded him in this research. Scattered at random throughout the early records were little slips of paper indicating pregnant sections. Briefly stated, they painted a picture somewhat as follows:

(a) The Original Meeting House burned to the ground some-where around 1793, but somehow the town clock was saved, at the expense of the rest of the building.

(b) The Shire built a new meeting house, but neglected to install the town clock, which spent the next 38 years in Sgt. Adams' barn.

(c) The church, which had shared the meeting house with the rest of the citizenry, wanted to build a proper church but coveted a site owned by the Shire.

(d) The Shire agreed to give the church the site it wanted, provided the church made provision to display the town clock.

(e) The church agreed to this, provided the Shire agreed to pay rent and maintain the clock.

(f) The Shire agreed to this condition, but only if the church would make the lower hall available for Shire functions occasionally.

(g) The church acceded to this modest request, provided that worldly uses not interfere with the regular profession of the Gospel.

(h) The Shire said O.K., because it didn't do much praying anyway.

Having ascertained the historical background that led to the incorporation of the town clock in the church in a manner that, on the face of it, didn't uncover any unseemly machinations on the part of either party, all that remained was for the Selectmen to put an article in the town warrant to raise the funds necessary for the repair job.

But just to be on the safe side, the Selectmen commissioned another survey of the clock and its supports, prepared by a group of church restorers who specialized in that sort of thing. These experts opined that all that was necessary was replacement of one beam-end that had been exposed to the weather, together with some new weather boards, the fastenings for which had just rusted away. The entire cost they said, would be somewhere around $1,472.86. The Selectmen questioned the 86¢, but on further reflection they began to ask themselves how the church people had come up with their $17,000 figure in the first place. Was it possible, the Selectmen wondered, that the Elders had in mind a modest profit for the church? This posed a definite challenge to the acumen of the Selectmen. If a group of psalm-singers could outsharp a cow farmer, a lumber dealer and a retired insurance adjuster, the country was in grave danger of disintegration. The issue could not go unchallenged, but it had to be joined in subtle fashion.

The Selectmen directed the Sexton of Cemeteries to cease and desist cranking up the weights that powered the town clock, as a result of which it stopped, making everyone in town late for whatever they intended to do in reliance on the town clock—including getting to church on time. This resulted in a definite slacking off of attendance, and consequently the gross amount of the offering. The parson delayed the offering until the end of the service in order to catch the late-comers, but it didn t do much to offset the shortfall.

The Parson then wanted to station the Sunday School Set in the vestibule to ring the Paul Revere bells, but the Selectmen stopped that right off the bat.

"If your belfry is in as bad shape as you say it is, we won't let you endanger our clock by ringing them bells," intoned the First Selectman.

Eventually the Selectmen inserted an item in the next town warrant to raise and appropriate enough money to repair the exposed beams in accordance with the recommendations of the church restorers, but not until an amendment was adopted, alleging high purposes, and reaffirming the sanctity of the doctrine of separation of church and state, along with a plea for nuclear disarmament. The Elders didn't question the modest size of the appropriation because the member of the choir who gave them their initial figure left town in the intervening time.

The beams were about to be replaced when some insurance type, also a member of the church, managed to sell both the church and the town on the need for a general liability policy covering the respective exposures of each group, by virtue of the hazardous nature of the work in question.

It would be nice of this saga could end right here, but it can't—and probably never will. The insurance company that issued the aforementioned policies, being somewhat at a loss to understand the nature of the relationships of the parties involved—both of which it appeared were insuring against each other—wanted covenants not to sue from both the town and the church.

The Selectmen refused to execute such a covenant, the effect of which would be to save the church harmless from all loss, on the ground that the church was execution-proof anyway and couldn't respond in damages if it had to.

The church, for its part, was willing to save the town harmless from loss on account of anything the church did, because it didn't plan to do anything anyway. But that was not what the insurance company wanted.

The insurance company then tried to cancel coverage for both the town and the church, but rescinded this action as a public relations gesture after receipt of a copy of a joint letter from the church and the town to the local newspaper, the original of which remains buried in Town Counsel's files because the original was never sent.

It is difficult to say when this will ever end. The Selectmen have advised town counsel to prepare an article for the next town warrant seeking authority to enter an agreement with the church by the terms of which the church will grant the town an easement and right of way over the church vestibule to enable the town officials to reach the town clock for the purposes of inspection, repair and adjustment.

The church indicated it might grant such an easement, but will offer an amendment describing the route of this easement and right of way. It will be up the back of the church, across the roof and then down the steeple to the clock.

An enduring exchange is in the making, one that promises to enliven town meetings for years to come, assuming the steeple doesn't collapse in the meantime.

# The Lumber Thief,
# Probable Cause and
# the Grange Whist Night

Legally speaking, municipal courts in our state are courts of original jurisdiction. Substitute the word "limited" for the word "original," and you've got it. Municipal courts on their own can deal with with civil matters where the amount of money in controversy is relatively trivial by today's standards.

On the criminal side, they deal with such weighty things as motor vehicle violations and the occasional assault and battery case, and conduct probable cause hearings on more serious offenses the police bring before them on the way to the state Superior Court. As such, they are somewhat like a one-man grand jury, responsible for saying "if you say so" to police allegations. In short, they have pretty wide scope, though it doesn't extend very far up the criminal ladder. It is the probable cause hearings that always generate interest, because the culprit is invariably in official police custody.

For years our local municipal court operated on a somewhat informal basis, holding forth in whatever room was available in the town hall. This was usually the Selectmen's room, reserved for court use whenever the Selectmen weren't using it. (Very few municipal courts enjoyed such amenities as dedicated courtrooms of their own.) The judge's chambers, or a conventional bench from which the judge could peer down menacingly at the assembled multitude, were luxuries enjoyed only by the Superior Court. This led to some pretty unconventional situations, to say the least.

The state troopers, whose function was to root out serious crime and bring it rapidly to justice, invariably began the process by taking their collar before the nearest municipal court for a probable cause hearing, a necessary preliminary to binding him over for trial before the state Superior Court. Because nobody could predict when a probable cause hearing might be required, they were invariably spur-of-the-moment affairs. The troopers were seldom able to schedule their arrests to coincide with regularly scheduled sessions of the municipal courts.

The case of the lumber thief was just such a case.

For several months, Philo Timmons, local sawmill operator, had complained of a shortage of logs on his skidway. He had tally sheets indicating the number of logs brought in, but somehow, between his skidway and his saw, the quantity seemed to shrivel up. He suspected log larceny, and complained to the local police who, upon visualizing a wave of rampant crime in the area, brought in the state troopers to handle the investigation.

It wasn't long before Trooper Bergeron, casually lolling about the piles of logs on Timmons' skidway late one night, saw a partially loaded logging truck come slowly down the road and back into Timmons' mill yard, ostensibly to unload its logs. But instead the driver, whose truck was equipped with a hydraulic cherry-picker, proceeded to top off his load with logs already on the skidway. Bergeron planned to nab him when he pulled out onto the public highway, but the driver didn't leave. He just climbed back into the cab of his truck and went to sleep.

Bergeron couldn't figure this out, and decided to stick around to see what else developed. He parked his cruiser in the shadows behind Timmons' planing mill, from where he could see the logging truck. He wanted to be on the scene with a clear view in case something else developed, but nothing did before he too dozed off.

About dawn the following morning when Bergeron awoke, the logging truck was still there with the driver still sleeping in the cab. Only when Timmons arrived to begin the day's sawing did the driver come to life. The truck remained only long enough to permit Timmons to take his tally of the logs as the driver unloaded them with the cherry picker.

It was obvious to Bergeron, if it wasn't to Timmons, that Timmons had just bought some of his own logs for the second and perhaps the third time around. Bergeron moved in and made the pinch.

That very evening the court convened in special session to deal with Trooper Bergeron's man, together with a domestic assault case that the local police, in the person of Chief Abernathy, had standing by. Trooper Bergeron asked for a 7 p.m. hearing, so he could file the guy away and still get home in time for supper with the wife and kids.

As luck would have it, word of the special session spread among the police of the surrounding towns, and they too showed up with a smattering of cases they wanted to dispose of before the weekend. The judge elected to handle them as his first order of business in order to have the decks clear for the log larceny matter, which was a case of some substance that required the undivided attention of the court.

Trooper Bergeron, not being particularly interested in standing guard over his prisoner, handcuffed him to one of the columns that hold up the second floor of the town hall, while he, Trooper Bergeron, assumed the position of a spectator in the courtroom, secure in the knowledge that his man wouldn't go anywhere without taking the town hall with him.

As things turned out, this was also whist night for the local grange, always held on the first floor of the town hall. The ladies of the grange arrived promptly at 7 p.m. Their husbands set up several card tables, and festivities got under way with coffee and dessert, which the handcuffed prisoner managed to share, albeit with some difficulty.

In order to deal with his repast, the log larcenist had the ladies shove one card table against the column he was cuffed to. Eventually the whist game got under way and the prisoner found himself overseeing the bidding of Mrs. Fred Pottle, an elderly, motherly and portly woman, who certainly needed his advice, since she was at the bottom of the ladder, whist-wise. He tried to introduce some life to the game by suggesting a small wager on behalf of Mrs. Pottle, but she figured he was in enough trouble as it was, so she cautioned against such a thing.

With the advice and suggestions of the culprit, Mrs. Pottle emerged as the high scorer in the first few rounds. Only when the court got around to his case did Trooper Bergeron go out to bring in his collar. He was met with loud protestations from Mrs. Pottle, who was just starting to enjoy her new-found expertise at whist. Furthermore, her husband had bet one of her famous apple pies with the master of the grange, and he didn't want to lose, which he surely would if the log larcenist was not available to counsel his wife. Pottle implored the court to "jest hold your horses for a while; this guy isn't going anywhere, and we need his advice."

The court, in all its majesty, said that justice couldn't loll about waiting for the whist game to end. The culprit had to appear, even if it meant Pottle's losing an apple pie to the master of the grange.

Various alternatives were explored, such as having the judge do his thing while the culprit remained handcuffed to the post, so the whist game not be unduly disrupted, but the judge rejected that idea, muttering something like "I don't play second fiddle to the grange whist club," a remark that was overheard by Mrs. Pottle, raising her hackles.

The matter was eventually sorted out, but not before Mrs. Pottle insisted on testifying as a character witness for the log larcenist, saying, "This man has enjoyed an impeccable reputation for as long as I've known him."

At the conclusion of the session, the judge enjoyed a slice of apple pie offered by the master of the grange.

# Town Meeting

In this day and age, when everything is getting bigger and more complex, and gov'mint is spreading like a plague across the land, it is a great relief to know that the last bulwark against this faceless monster is still the typical New England Town Meeting, which permits one and all to pound away at the bureaucratic incursions with a form of government that hasn't changed appreciably in the past couple of hundred years.

While the cast of characters may have changed, and some of the legendary performers at Town Meeting now gaze up from the quiet of the cemetery behind the town hall to bemoan their mealy-mouthed, spineless successors, on the whole the show continues to play out as it always has in the past. Every single registered voter with strength enough to climb the stairs to the meeting hall, and endurance enough to outlast his neighbors, can have his say on whatever triviality bothers him the most about how the town conducts its business.

For example, a typical exchange might run like this:

A suave, recently arrived taxpayer, who is also the Third Assistant Vice-President, Finance, of an electronic firm in Nashua, speaks in support of a hairy scheme by which the town can save money over the long run by buying road salt in bulk in concert with other towns, if enough is ordered to add up to 10,000 tons in one shot.

This proposal is countered by the road agent, who might suggest that he'd "go along with the idea, if the proposer could suggest just where he is proposing to store such a quantity of salt, because the total storage capacity I have is only 50 tons. And the total consumption of all the towns in the district is only 1,200 tons a winter anyhow. Is the taxpayer suggesting that we erect a $40,000 storage building in order to save $800 a year? If my figures are correct, we might just break even in about 50 years!"

"While I have the greatest respect for your professional abilities as road agent, I'm afraid you have failed to appreciate the parameters upon which my model is built," retorts the Third Assistant Vice-President for Finance.

His analysis is choked off by Cyrus Whipple, who rises and shouts, "I'm for the road agent. He keeps my road plowed out in winter, and my old truck ain't all ate out with with no road salt neither." Amid shouts of "Forget it" and "Let's move on to something sensible" from the spectators in the back rows, the matter is dropped.

No vote is ever taken on such schemes because the Moderator, having perceived the sense of the meeting just by listening to the ebb and flow of the exchanges from the floor, adroitly moves on to the next item on the agenda—to which, in this case, the Third Assistant Vice-President, Finance, objects.

"I'd like to have my objection noted in the record," says the Third Assistant Vice-President, Finance, to which the Moderator replies, "We'll send you a letter."

"Please do, just for my records, you know," retorts the Third Assistant Vice-President, Finance, who then gets up and leaves the meeting in a snit, amid loud cheering, which he attributes to widespread support.

Every year a smattering of newspaper reporters from as far away as Boston show up for Town Meeting to memorialize the proceedings for posterity. They invariably pound out damp, moist-eyed pieces extolling the manifold virtues of the little republics in the hinterlands, and bemoan the day—not far off in their judgment—when all this will be a thing of the past. To the casual observer, unfamiliar with the durability of local institutions and the people who run them, it might be easy to get the idea that rugged individualism went the way of the New Deal, and that what remains is but a vestige of its former splendor.

Little do they know that our version of participatory government has been going on for years and years, and is not apt to falter on the rocks and shoals of the latest outpourings from Washington or anywhere else. On the contrary, it is very much alive and continually takes on new vigor, gaining strength with each new regulation.

This is due in no small way to the fact that the institution of Town Meeting seems to propagate its own personality. Some say it acts as an antibody to all outside regulation, whatever its source. The fact that in the past twenty or so years the town has grown materially, and there are now more new people than old-timers, hasn't made the slightest difference in the proceedings.

A man may have moved here from New York, Arizona, or even Connecticut, and whether he's a retired steam fitter or an inside commodities trader, once he's in Town Meeting, he's more apt than not to jump up and yell, "Mr. Moderator—MISTER Moderator—MISTER MODERATOR, DAMMIT!" and then demand the floor, to the complete mystification of his family and friends, to harangue the meeting for several minutes in a fashion that startles even himself, once the enormity of his act begins to sink in.

Men whose sole public utterances have been the recitation of the Lord's Prayer on Sunday blossom out as orators in the style of William Jennings Bryan delivering his famous "Cross of Gold" speech. The times may have changed, and the cast of characters may have changed, but Town Meeting remains the same.

As a rule, the polished newcomers in their gray flannel trousers, blue blazers and tasseled Gucci loafers take seats about a third of the way from the front rows, leaving the first six or eight rows empty. This is because they want to be seen entering by those in the rear of the hall, yet not wind up so far down front that they are in any danger of being called upon to act as tally clerks for any votes that may occur.

At the rear of the hall, filling the back row of benches, leaning up against the walls and choking off the entrance, can be found a group of citizens difficult to classify. Among them can be found the few remaining farmers in town, who have come to the meeting after milking their cows, along with an assortment of loggers, wood-choppers and reporters from Boston.

Sprinkled throughout the audience are the outright argumentative people, who have come solely to keep the Selectmen on their toes. Their forces are occasionally augmented by the truly bewildered, the righteously indignant, and a couple of self-styled straight thinkers who arise only when the arguments appear to have strayed too far afield for their tastes, and who seek to gather all this together in the form of a lengthy statement only marginally related to the question before the house—which everyone has forgotten anyway. These are the people who invariably resort to some hair-splitting distinction, just, as they invariably say, "… to make sure everyone is straight in their thinking," which nobody is, including the current thinking-straightener.

Up on the stage, smiling benevolently out over the heads of the throng, are the three Selectmen, along with the Moderator, the purportedly impartial referee who presides over the meeting. Good Moderators are like the end-men in a minstrel show; they try to keep things moving with a semblance of order. There are those who say Moderators are only partially impartial, but the extent of their impartiality depends on their ability to get the sense of the meeting, an ability said to be inherited, not native to the breed. If they were truly impartial, the first Town Meeting would still be going on.

Occasionally Moderators are tempted to innovate, and when they do, chaos reigns. One spin of this wheel that never fails to confuse the voters is the practice of voting not on the article before the

house, but on the recommendation of the Ways and Means
Committee. This tends to get sticky when the Ways and Means
Committee recommends voting against the article as it appears in
the warrant, in which case a "yes" vote on the recommendation is
really a "no" vote on the article.

For example, if the warrant article seeks to raise and appropriate
$100 in support of the Merrimac Valley Regional Association,
and the Ways and Means Committee thinks this is a pretty ques-
tionable cause, it will recommend against the article. The
Moderator will then intone, "The vote will be on the recommendation of the Ways and Means Committee. Are you ready for the
question?"

Chorus of voices: NO! NO! NO!

Lady in mink coat: Does that mean if we want to vote yes for the
appropriation, we have to vote no on this Ways and Means thing?

Moderator: Yes.

Lady in mink coat: For yes we should vote no, or yes we should
vote yes?

Retired Navy officer: Mister Moderator, perhaps I can straighten
out everyone's thinking on this issue. If you want to vote against
the recommendation of the Ways and Means Committee, which
itself recommends against the article, then you should vote yes on
the article, and no on the recommendation; is that clear? (Pause)
In other words, if you wish to override the recommendation
which opposes the article ... sorry, I got that backwards. IF you

want to vote against the Ways and Means Committee report, then you should vote yes on the article; is that clear?

Moderator: Commander, you may be on the right course, but you're certainly in the wrong ocean. A vote on the recommendation of Ways and Means ...

Voice from the rear of the hall: EVERYONE WHO WANTS TO GIVE AWAY A HUNDRED BUCKS SAY YES. ( A smattering of yeas and nays are heard here and there in the room.)

Moderator: The nays have it. Now to article five of the warrant.

Chairman of the PTA: Mister Moderator, what did we just do?

Moderator: Lady, who am I to question the inscrutable ways of Providence?

Sometimes Providence doesn't bother to intervene at all. When that happens, towns have been known to proceed in such confusion that the records reveal they have done such things as (a) vote to secede from Hillsborough County, (b) vote in favor of China's nuclear policy, and (c) vote down the entire town budget. People may wonder how government can run at all in such circumstances, but it does so very simply by ignoring the votes completely, and then passing another one at the next Town Meeting to correct the records to conform to what the Selectmen have actually done in the meantime.

Town budgets are always a source of extended argument. The Selectmen invariably craft a budget they think is appropriate to run the town for the next year, including a modest cushion. Unfortunately, they're the only ones that think it is appropriate, and lively debate follows their attempts to get it passed in bulk. There is always someone who raises the specter of the line-item veto, a device that enables the assembled citizenry to take the budget apart, item by item.

The Selectmen, anticipating this attack annually, have adopted the practice of loading up the Ways and Means Committee with a majority of newcomers to town, who because they have come from areas accustomed to spending money like there is no tomorrow, have a tendency to view the Selectmen's budget as downright penurious, and frequently increase it. The Selectmen then toss the ball back to the Ways and Means Committee, which winds up doing battle for them. When the dust finally settles, the budget is apt to be cut, but it is still larger than the Selectmen regard as absolutely necessary for the town to function at all.

A few years ago Dutch Elm Disease began to attack some of the stately old elms on the village green, and the question arose as to how to deal with the problem. Amherst without its elms would certainly be less attractive, some said, but they were at a loss to know what to do about it. The issue was raised in Town Meeting under the "any other business to come before the town" provision in the warrant for the meeting.

Tentative opinions seemed to get nowhere, and the Town Tree Committee, consisting of six taxpayers, three from the village and the other three from outlying areas, was duly appointed by the

Moderator to look into the matter and report back at the next Town Meeting.

The following year the Committee reported back, saying it needed an appropriation of $1,500 to hire an arborist to advise them.

Ezekiel Tomkins rose in opposition, saying all the Committee had to do was call the forestry department at the State University, which would be glad to provide the technical support and advice for free. "No need to spend all that money hiring experts when the University men are already being paid by the State," he pointed out.

The Committee hung its head in shame for failing to appreciate and take advantage of this resource which they were already paying for anyway. Another year passed, during which two more elms fell victim to disease.

The following year the Committee rendered its then current report, the impact of which was that while certain delaying tactics could be employed to postpone the effects of the infection, in the final analysis little could be done to stem the onslaught of Dutch Elm Disease, short of cutting down all the elms on the village green. The town was asked to recall the demise of the chestnut trees, which virtually disappeared from New England years ago due to some similar ailment. The Committee did, however, recommend that immediate steps be taken to cut down all the diseased elms still standing to prevent the spread of the disease to those trees that appeared healthy, a proposal that was supported by the loggers attending the meeting.

Ezekiel again rose in opposition, saying denuding the center of town was a stupid move, since all the surrounding woods were full of elms, most of which were probably infected too. "Unless you cut down every elm in the entire town, you'll never stop the spread of the damned thing," he said.

Colonel Rufus Smith, USAF (Ret.), a newcomer to town, suggested that maybe it would be better if the Tree Committee were renamed the Reforestation Committee, and henceforth devoted its efforts to replacing the dead elms with something more hardy, like maples.

The Tree Committee, now redesignated the Reforestation Committee by acclamation, then moved to appropriate the sum of $5,000 for the purchase and planting of maples around the village green.

Ezekiel Tomkins gave an impassioned speech in support of the appropriation, an action totally out of character for him, since he usually opposed anything that might raise his taxes. When questioned after the meeting, he said, "Why wouldn't I support something that will improve the appearance of the town? I'm selling out and going to Florida, and until I get my price, I don't want the center of town looking like a bomb crater."

New England Yankees, if nothing else, reveal a certain practicality in their doings that even the likes of Calvin Coolidge would appreciate.

# Getting Back to Basics:
# the Resurrection
# of the Town Dump

According to Fleepsie Snapser, mother of four, chairperson of the PTA and dutiful wife of C. Wesley Snapser, living in Amherst is like living in the Garden of Eden, and she should know; she's pregnant again.

Hiram Hepplewhite, the present holder of the Boston Globe Cane, awarded annually to the oldest mobile resident of town, views Amherst in a somewhat different light. Hiram says that when Adam decided to have a go at Eve, he shucked his fig leaf and just tossed it aside. By that very act of environmental indifference, he created the Amherst Town Dump. Hiram says that's the only connection he can think of between Amherst and the Garden of Eden.

Nobody really knows when the Town Dump was actually begun. The local archeological society, which for years has conducted digs at the dump, contends that its origins are buried deep in antiquity. The society maintains an exhibit at the library of artifacts its members have unearthed at the dump as proof of this assertion. Hiram says that doesn't prove anything, other than that garbage is timeless.

The thing that nobody has been able to fathom is why, if the dump is so old, it didn't burst its bounds long ago. The town has experienced uncontrolled growth over the last fifteen years, and is again approaching the population it had in the early eighteen hundreds. Yet the Town Dump just soldiered along, consuming whatever the citizens fed it, steadfastly remaining within its original ten acres. It therefore came as both a shock and a surprise when a group of environmental activists raised a hue and cry that the Town Dump had to be closed.

"With the vast increases in the population of the town, together with our changing lifestyles, we have to prepare for the future," they chorused.

"The only solution is to establish a sanitary landfill, if we are to avoid being engulfed in our own trash. That old man who runs the dump—Tuttle, I think his name is—can't possibly cope much longer. He's just not technologically sophisticated enough to handle the trash of the future," added one.

That remark, uttered at an informal meeting of the Ad Hoc Committee to Review Trash Disposal Alternatives, by one who Titus "Tiny" Tuttle referred to as "One o' them thar suede-shoe, button-down-collar fellas," raised Tiny's hackles. Tiny held hereditary dump-picking rights at the Town Dump.

"As a hereditary dump-picker, I got my rights handed down to me by my Pa, and he got 'em handed down to him from his'n too. Ain't never been a time when my kin didn't have dump-pickin rights to this here old town dump. Why, we been pickin' this dump for at least four generations 'til this bastard showed up. If'n it weren't for him, there'd be no complaints from nobody. And furthermore, we don't cost the town nothin neither," Tiny said, hitting what some people regarded as a responsive chord.

Actually, there had been no complaints about the Town Dump or Tiny's services. The Ad Hoc Committee to Review Trash Disposal Alternatives was created when too many people were appointed to the Culvert and Catch Basin Committee, and something had to be found for them to do. There wasn't enough wrong with the local culverts and catch basins to occupy them, so they turned their attention to the Town Dump.

The dump, however, had been trouble-free for as long as anyone could recall, functioning on a mix of local initiatives that kept it out of the limelight, among them being what is probably the oldest form of recycling extant in the nation.

Because the town had no regular trash pickup service, everyone had to take their junk to the dump, which did its best business on weekends, when all the husbands were at home. Typically on Saturday they would pile the week's accumulation of trash and garbage in the family station wagon, along with the kids and the dog, ostensibly to take the trash directly to the dump. This was the theory anyway, but as things turned out, the husbands would first cruise around town visiting their friends and acquaintances, and at each top everyone would inspect each other's load, some portion of which they invariably coveted. What was one fellow's sow's ear was his neighbor's silk purse.

"Cedric, you're not taking that old TV to the dump, are you? If you are, I'll relieve you of the burden right now. I'm an electronic engineer, you know, and I can probably fix it up for my mother-in-law and get her off my back for a while."

"Be my guest, Claude, but it won't be for free. You'll have to give me those two old kitchen cabinets you've ripped out. I need something like that for my shop in the barn. If we just off-load right here, I can pick up the cabinets on my way back from the dump. On second thought, with all that bulk gone, why don't we consolidate our loads, and take only one car to the dump?"

With that sort of recycling, very little of the big stuff ever made it to the dump at all. It just moved around town to begin life anew at someone else's house.

The second significant environmental process that kept the Town Dump within bounds was Tiny Tuttle. In his capacity as hereditary dump picker, he had first dibs on everything arriving at the dump. Tiny specialized in plumbing fixtures, cast-off appliances, antiques and children's toys and furniture. His counterpart at the Mont Vernon Dump handled bottles, cans and bric-à-brac. The dump picker at the Hollis Dump concentrated on batteries, old tires and building rubble. Between them they accounted for the bulk of the heavy stuff that, but for their services, would have wound up in their respective dumps.

Tiny used to park his beat-up old pickup truck at the brow of our Town Dump, from where he could scope out each car as it backed up to unload. He'd then intercept not only those items he specialized in, but also those his counterparts at the other dumps handled. On Sunday night, they'd all meet at one dump or the other, and exchange what they didn't specialize in for what they did, enabling each of them to make one stop on Monday morning at the particular salvage yard that also specialized in what each of them had on board. What the salvage yards didn't take went into inventory for resale to the less fortunate in Nashua. In short, what the dump pickers didn't take went over the brow into the dump, and being mostly garbage, the woodchucks made short work of it, converting it to benign compost.

Tiny had another very useful function. Occasionally some resident would wheel into the dump, back up a bit to enthusiastically, and immediately get himself bogged down in loose garbage. Tiny would then get out his chain, squirm through the garbage under the front of the car and hook up the chain, so the Road Agent could haul the car out with the road grader. This was a very handy function, especially for those who came from urban areas, and who lacked experience in where the ground ended and the garbage began.

It therefore came as quite a surprise when the Ad Hoc Committee to Review Trash Disposal Alternatives aggressively insisted on pursuing the notion that the old Town Dump had to be closed in favor of their scheme, a sanitary landfill.

"The sanitary landfill concept is state of the art, technologically speaking, and will meet our trash disposal needs for the foreseeable future," the chairman intoned. When the foreseeable future turned out to be no further down the road than the blink of an eye—14 years to be exact—the following article appeared in the Town Warrant:

"ARTICLE 16: To see if the town will vote to take a sum equal to 25% of the current user fees up to a maximum of $100,000 to be set aside in a special fund towards the eventual closing of the landfill or take action relative thereto."

It passed.

As is frequently the case when ancient institutions such as the Town Dump are supplanted by so-called modern technology, trivial but absolutely vital considerations are swept aside in the rush to embrace the new technology. Obviously, something of the sort caused the new sanitary landfill to burst its bounds in the bloom of its youth, and I wanted to find out what it was, by calling on Richard "Red" Macomber, the Road Agent, at his office in the Town Barn, which was itself located on the site of the old Town Dump. Unfortunately, I never made it to the Town Barn. The entire area encompassing both the Town Dump and the Town Barn was surrounded by a high chain-link fence, along which signs were posted, saying

KEEP OUT—HAZARDOUS WASTES

This was enough to give anyone pause, and raised serious questions of how anyone like me, a long-time patron of the old Town Dump, had managed to make it this far, especially if those signs were correct.

I eventually found Red bent over a computer in his new office in the Town Hall, trying to figure out the cost of digging up the entire sanitary landfill, and shipping the contents off to somewhere in Utah.

"Red," I asked, "What happened? I understood the sanitary landfill was the answer to a maiden's prayer. Wasn't it supposed to last well into the next century, or are people making more trash than they used to?"

"No," he said, "people aren't making more trash. It's just that we have to handle it differently now that Tiny Tuttle is banned, and the hours have been changed. Why don't you look up old Tiny; he can fill you in on what has happened better than I can. He still lives out on the old Brookline Road. Anyway, he has the only solution to the whole mess."

Tiny lives "over the store," as they say, in a combination house and warehouse complex, consisting of a series of connected chicken houses, sheds and lean-tos, around which he has accumulated an enormous inventory of old plumbing fixtures, pipes, refrigerators, washers and dryers and related items too numerous to mention. Several vintage pickup trucks lay about in various stages of disrepair. Chickens called an old Cadillac home. A typical junkyard dog was chained up, near what appeared to be the only means of access to the place. Several slightly soiled children were running about, being chased by a well-worn woman in a Mother Hubbard.

"Is Mr. Tuttle at home?" I asked.

"Yup," she replied.

"Well, would it be possible for me to speak to him?" I inquired.

"Not if'n he don't wanna talk to you," she responded, adding, "But I'll ask 'im. TINY, THEY'S A FELLOW IN A COAT AN' TIE WANTS TO TALK TO YOU," she shouted, as she grabbed one of the children who happened to come within range.

After a few minutes, Tiny appeared, put the junkyard dog in the cab of an old pickup truck which I vaguely thought I recognized, and said, "Whadda want?"

"Well, you may not remember me, but I used to live in town. Met you some years ago when you managed the old town dump," I said, adding, "I represented you once a number of years ago when you had a little problem with the local police—DWI, if I recall."

"Oh, yas, now I remember. You didn't charge me nothin', but then you didn't lose your license neither. Yas, I sure do remember you," he said, with what struck me as a rather petulant tone of voice.

He waved at me to follow him into one of the chicken houses. "Careful," he said, "hen shit ate out the underpin'ns, and I ain't had no time to fix 'em, what with runnin' the Hereditary Dump Picker's Society, you know. Now that that damned landfill is about to be closed, we figure we have a chance to get the old town dump opened up again and get back our rights to pick it. Ours is the only environmentally sound solution, but we have to sell it, you unnerstan'. I been workin' on the publicity."

After passing through a succession of connecting chicken houses filled with a vast assortment of appliances and parts, we arrived at Tiny's office, which had been a grain room in better times. Tiny directed me to take a seat on what remained of an old Lawson sofa, which I vaguely recognized as having been lugged to the dump by a neighbor many years ago. As I sank back in the Lawson, a cloud of grain dust arose, briefly obscuring my vision.

When the dust finally settled and my vision cleared, Tiny was seated on what had been a swivel chair, which was now attached to the top of a 40-quart milk jug with two bent nails. His desk featured several cut-off beer cans with the tops bent over to form futuristic ash trays. He cleared the top of his desk with a sweep of his arm, sending the ash trays and several chicks flying.

Tiny began the conversation by asking, "You're not from the state, are ya, cuz if'n y'are, git lost. I ain't got no license, an' I ain't about to apply for none. I'm an en-tray-pren-oor now, and we don't need no licenses to do nothin," he said.

"No, I'm not from the state. I just learned that you're no longer in charge of things at the landfill, and I was wondering whether you're retired, or what."

"No, I'm not retired and I still own my hereditary dump-pickin rights. If the plan we Hereditary Dump Pickers have works, I'll be back at my old stand by spring, ya know. Wanna hear about our plan?" he asked.

"That's why I sought you out, Tiny. Red says you have the only viable plan available. Naturally I want he hear about it," I said, hoping to encourage him, which turned out to be unnecessary. Tiny had a captive audience, and he was not about to be put off.

"Wal, we have a two-pronged attack. First, when garbage piles up all over town after the landfill is closed, and people begin to move away to escape the stench, we'll offer to git rid of it if'n the town will reopen the old Town Dump. Then we'll keep it closed during the week and open it only on weekends. With the dump open only on Saturday and Sunday, the husbands'll have to make the dump run, and before long, visitin' around town and exchangin' the heavy stuff with each other will start up again. That way, the stuff actually going to the dump'll be little more than what we hereditary dump pickers useta handle. That'll settle source recycling for a fair-thee-well," he said.

"But Tiny, I heard you were banned from the landfill. How do you plan to handle things at the dump? Won't the thing that got you banned raise its ugly head again?"

"Naw, that happened at the landfill when I squirmed under some dame's car to hook up my chain when she backed up too far and got stuck in the garbage. She thought I was making obscene gestures at her while I was doin' that, and she had me banned. That can't happen at the old town dump, because it won't be open during the week and the women won't be making the dump run. With the husbands doin' the dump run on weekends, I doubt I'll have any problems," he said, with assurance.

That was certainly an unassailable argument. But could Tiny handle the increased volume, now that the town had grown? He had an answer for that too.

"As I said, I got my hereditary dump-pickin' rights handed down to me from my Pa, an' I plan to hand 'em down to my kids too. I got four boys and two girls, so we oughta be able to handle the increase. May have to put 'nother truck on the road, but I've got plenty of 'em I can fix up. Anyway, I'm goin' to go from a boutique picker to a volume picker, and we need the volume to make a day's pay. Can't fail," he concluded.

"But Tiny, what about the garbage? The environmentalists will surely oppose anything that doesn't involve addressing their concerns, won't they?"

"No, not when they unnerstan' our game plan. Once the old town dump is open, the woodchucks'll return, and we got more woodchucks aroun' here'n people. One good woodchuck'll compost a whole bag of garbage a night. Anyway, we've got the garden club behind us, 'cause they want the compost for the flower beds aroun' the village green. It's all just gettin' back to basics, if you know what I mean," he said. "Once we work off the backlog that'll pile up when the landfill is shut down, and we hereditary dump pickers get back to our old stands, everythin'll be fine. After all, the old town dump been aroun' 190 years, give or take, without bustin' its bounds, all because of generations of us dedicated hereditary dump pickers, with some help from the woodchucks."

"Sounds good to me, Tiny, but have you got much local support for your plan?" I asked.

"We sure do. The Selectmen are for it, because the town won't havta spend a fortune every year like they do now on the landfill. That thing costs a couple of hundred grand a year. The Overseer of the Poor is for it, 'cause with all us workin', me and my family can get off relief. The wives around town are for it, 'cause they won't have to make the dump run any more. The husbands are for it, 'cause they can use up an entire weekend just goin' to the dump. About the only one agin' it is the guy trying to sell the town on an incinerator, but he won't get very far. The fire department is agin' it as a fire hazard during the dry season. They's a lot of things going for us, you know."

As Tiny says, it's just a matter of getting back to basics.

# Changing
# Times

In the boom years following World War II, our town grew rapidly. People from such foreign lands as Dallas, New York and Los Angeles wound up selecting Amherst as the place to live, when they came east to staff the burgeoning electronics industry that bloomed along Route 128 outside Boston. Nobody knows what aimed them at Amherst, but coming as they did from urban areas, they viewed the asking prices for the better places around town as dirt cheap.

"Where else can you find an eleven-room classic Colonial, completely restored, right smack in the center of a picture-book town at a price that is a steal?" they'd say to their friends.

Only after they realized that the prices they paid were the outlandishly high asking prices the natives always start out with, on the theory that you can always come down, but you can never go up, did they realize that maybe they had been taken in.

Furthermore, the first few places that sold for these high prices encouraged other locals to put their places on the market so they too could cash in while the market was hot.

"I'm selling out before someone finds out," the more crafty among them was heard to say, when asked why he contemplated such a move, when his family had lived in the same place for four generations. "We may be slow learners, but we eventually catch on," they'd say.

But gradually awakening to what was going on didn't slow the price escalation one bit. Newcomers began to encourage others to make the same mistake they did, and before long, the level of asking prices ratcheted upward still further. Nobody wanted to admit he made a mistake, especially when he could persuade someone else to do the same thing, thereby reinforcing the validity of the new level of prices he himself had helped create. If enough people thought the prices were low, they were low, even though they were high. As one newcomer who bought early said, "It's all relative, you know?"

With all this frantic activity, the supply of old brick-end Colonials ran out, along with the clapboard ones too. Sensing an unfulfilled market, local cow farmers became developers and built new old Colonials by the dozen. New subdivisions sprang up in the flood plain and on the tops of hills, where they had to drill through 1,100 feet of granite, at eight bucks a foot, just to get a teacup of water. With demand at an all-time high, the locals continued to be intent on cashing in while the market was hot. Before it all leveled out, the population of the town grew from 856 in 1950 to around 12,000 today.

But that's not the point of this story. With all the new people moving into town and entitled to vote in town affairs, they couldn't all fit in the meeting room on the second floor of the town hall. The town couldn't afford to build a new and bigger town hall because it was sorely taxed just to provide schools for the newly arrived propagators. They had paid so much for their houses that they were short of cash and had to rely on an old-fashioned form of recreation that they could indulge in right in their own bedrooms, thereby adding to the problem. Quite naturally, this required ever larger schools, all of which had large gymnasiums. The gymnasiums provided the solution to the cramped town hall, but also gave rise to the difficulty about to be revealed.

To accommodate the crowds attending Town Meeting, the town decided to hold it in the gym at the newest school. Certainly the place was large enough—some said cavernous—to handle those attending the meeting, including the King's Daughters, who elected to hold their annual bake sale in the rear.

The problem developed because of the very size and volume of the space. Petite members of the Village Birdwatchers' Society couldn't be heard at all without a megaphone. Shouts of LOUDER, LOUDER were heard all over the hall. Furthermore, in contentious matters, where everyone wanted to talk at once, nothing could be accomplished over the hubbub. Something had to be done to avert total chaos.

Fortunately the town was blessed with an inordinate number of electrical engineers, all of whom volunteered their professional expertise to develop a sound system that would enable people to be heard. The problem was that each of them approached the problem from a different direction.

The Selectmen, being beyond their collective depth with anything more complex than changing a lightbulb, adopted the time-honored course of appointing a Committee of the Whole to look into the matter, and report back at the next Town Meeting. This had the effect of sweeping all the available talent into the project, and incidentally assured the Committee of everlasting life.

During the summer recess when the school was closed, it was nevertheless alive with all sorts of people stringing wires around the gym, each in support of a different system. One system was so effective, it could be heard outside the school. Testing, testing, testing—one, two three, became the standard fare for the neighbors.

Several weeks before the next Town Meeting, the Selectmen were called upon to choose one of the four or five systems the Committee had developed. The one they selected involved some sort of control panel that the Selectmen could manage, together with a device called a mixer, whose purpose completely mystified them.

Running down the center isle were four wires, each to be connected to a microphone presided over at the meeting by an usher, whose job it was to deliver the microphone to whoever stood up wanting to talk. The other three microphones could be cut off at the control box, so that only the selected speaker could enjoy the sound of his or her voice booming out throughout the room. At least that was the theory of the thing.

But this system didn't work out very well. As the microphone was being passed along the row to the speaker, everyone handling it took the opportunity to put in two cents worth.

"Since I have the microphone, I just want to remind the members that the PTA career night panel will hold an organizational meeting at Fleepsie Snapser's house this Friday. Fleepsie will have the coffee on, but bring your own snacks. This will be a working meeting."

Interjections of this sort were typical in an argument before the house on whether to buy a new road grader of just fix the old one. Things became even more complex when the person with the microphone wanted to ask the previous speaker just who he thinks he is, causing the person across the isle to demand the microphone for a rebuttal.

Before long, the entire system was caught up in an electronically amplified argument among people on the floor, which the Moderator managed to cut short simply by turning the entire system off, in favor of recognizing whoever he felt like recognizing and hoping for the best.

The following year a somewhat different system was tried out, one in which a single microphone was set up in the center of the room. Anyone wishing to speak had to line up at the podium to which the mike was attached. This system proved unworkable because everyone shouted into the thing at once; the resulting din was totally unintelligible.

Some thought was given to requiring anyone who wished to speak to submit his or her question in writing so the speaker could be recognized in turn. This idea didn't even survive its first test when one habitually vocal citizen asked, "How in hell can I write a question until I know what the rest of you nuts are going to say?" This made sense to the Selectmen, so they abandoned the written question routine, leaving them right back at square one.

At last report, the Grange had established a new tradition in town by selling little cardboard megaphones at the door, the proceeds going to support the Reforestation Committee. The Moderator borrowed the athletic coach's large megaphone, so now everyone is on a par.

Until the electronic types get their act sorted out, the neighborhood will just have to live with the screeches and howls floating from the gym on weekends, as they try yet another approach.

# Bad Karma
# and the Primal
# Scream Center

For the longest time the locals thought we were immune to the ills of such places as New York, Berkeley and Woodstock, where vast hordes of indigents undertook to propagate in corn fields, under cover of clouds of pot smoke. Oh, we had a few home-grown kooks, a small contingent of Moonies, and a few less well defined neer-do-wells, but they wouldn't have amounted to very much in any age. Most of them eventually tired of just hanging around and got jobs working for the town, cleaning out catch basins and clearing brush at intersections.

Then it happened. A complacent town was brought sharply to attention when the Biddle sisters, a couple of old maids living near the former Frankie Blackwell chicken-plucking plant, reported hearing a series of piercing screams coming from the abandoned pluckery. Not only that, several people, returning to town from the late shift down in Nashua, said weird, flashing, colored lights had been seen through windows on the lower level of the plant down near the river. Modest efforts by the police to investigate the reports hadn't produced much of anything, one way or the other, and the whole thing just sort of petered out, unresolved.

What brought it all to a head was a late night call from Hattie Biddle, the elder of the two sisters, to the communications center at the police station, reporting that a naked man, covered with blood, had just run through her yard screaming bloody murder.

"He's heading for town, but I doubt that he'll make it," she said, adding, "He can't possibly live very long, bleeding the way he is."

A short time later, Officer Tweedy, on foot patrol on the village green, saw a naked man, screaming and bleeding profusely, head for the horse-watering trough beside the green and plunge right in, head first. Tweedy had visions of being in on the last convulsions of a dying man, and called for a backup.

When everyone got the victim back to the station house, Doc Tribble, the local medico, after what was thought to be a pretty cavalier examination, reported that there was nothing whatsoever wrong with the fellow. He was just covered from head to foot with ketchup and pasta sauce.

"Hose him down, and then maybe we can get to the bottom of all this, but I think he's just plain nuts," Doc opined.

Officer Tweedy was directed to take the ketchup and pasta man out back and do as Doc suggested.

"I don't want to smear up the new paint in the holding pen with all that goo that's on him," the Police Chief commented, as he mobilized his forces for the purpose of really scouting out the chicken-plucking plant.

Upon their arrival at the pluckery, the forces of law and order found a group of about a dozen or more people covered in red sheets, sitting in a circle on the floor of the eviscerating room, swaying back and forth.

The remains of the last lot of birds to go through the place, though somewhat the worse for wear, passed slowly before the group, the conveyor having been turned on.

The whole scene was lit by flashing colored lights reflected off a round, mirrored globe that hung from the ceiling, much like the one that hangs from the ceiling of the Baboosic Lake Ballroom, intended to give a surrealistic aura to an otherwise pretty drab scene.

Suddenly the entire group began to scream, jump up and run around the eviscerating room in a collective frenzy before finally falling to the floor prostrate, as the screaming subsided, giving way to moaning and crying. A pretty bizarre display for Milford.

Back at the police station, the ketchup and pasta man, having been hosed down by Officer Tweedy and told, "Don't you move a God-damned inch 'til I find you some pants," began to feel the bite of the cool night air. Being without clothes, he took refuge in the cellar of the town hall and put on the only thing he could find—an old police reserve uniform he found hanging in the locker room.

Ignoring Tweedy's directive, he headed back to the chicken-plucking plant, where he intended to resume doing whatever it was he was doing before the unscheduled events of the past hour overtook him.

On his arrival, the Police Chief mistook him for a member of the reserve force, and ordered him to remain at the plant to stand guard over the evidence while the rest of the posse took the red-sheet contingent back to the station house for booking.

The records are bare of what transpired next, but the memory of those involved tends to indicate the following circumstances:

The group in custody were part of a new spiritual awakening scheme, based on the curative effects of group indulgence in primal scream therapy. It was led by Swami Vishkanu Vivikananadi, an Indian mystic with long, stringy hair, a lush beard and piercing black eyes, who insisted that was his real name, though he may have been somebody else in another life.

The group had appropriated the chicken-plucking plant, which had been closed for a year or more, due to the fact that Doc Tribble closed it down when he learned Frankie Blackwell was discharging the viscera from operations right into the Souhegan River, where they piled up against the dam downstream, causing an awful smell.

A further and perhaps more cogent reason for the primal screamers to choose the chicken-plucking plant as the site of their Northern New England branch, was that it was easy to enter and leave without attracting attention. All the new converts had to do was wade across the river from the Amherst side and then climb in any one of the broken windows on the lower level of the building.

The group was engaged in an organizational and membership meeting, when it was interrupted first by the escape of a new member, and then by the police. The Chief lectured the Swami on the evils of trespass on other people's property, but the Swami just shrugged.

"We are citizens of the universe," he said, "and we just made use of what you worldly people abandoned. You may not believe it, but several of our converts are serving in the Peace Corps at this very moment."

The very thought that the nation's foreign relations might be in the hands of the Swami's disciples was disquieting.

As things appeared to be getting nowhere, the Swami insisted on calling his attorney, who materialized shortly thereafter in the form of Ms. Hester Andretti-Boggs, a local lawyer who specialized in women's causes and whatever nobody else would handle, including things like the Swami and his predicament.

Hester showed up in sandals, long braids and a Mother Hubbard dress, accompanied by the local representative of the Civil Liberties Union. They immediately insisted the the Swami and his flock be charged or released.

"This thing has all the earmarks of a major civil liberties case," the CLU man said, "and I intend to press it to the hilt—including suing for false arrest."

This unnerved the Police Chief, since he had the entire group handcuffed together, with the last man on each end of the line cuffed to the railing outside the police station. They were all squatting cross-legged on the sidewalk, slowly swaying back and forth, chanting in some unintelligible tongue.

The Chief ordered them released, a small risk since they weren't apt to get very far unnoticed while they were dressed in red sheets. He figured that even if they took them off, they'd be even more noticeable. But he had to charge someone with something if the whole show wasn't to become a complete washout.

It then occurred to him that maybe the ketchup man was the key to the whole thing. At least he was guilty of lewd and lascivious behavior, no matter how you looked at it.

"Tweedy, bring up your collar," directed the Chief. Tweedy went down to the holding pen, but returned to report sheepishly that the ketchup man had escaped. At least he was nowhere to be found.

It was only after the Chief sent a contingent back to the chicken-plucking plant to secure the premises, such as it was, that the ketchup man was located, still dressed in the old police reserve uniform, dutifully standing guard over the eviscerating line. He was returned to the police station in handcuffs.

Unfortunately there is no record of any court proceedings resulting from the evening's activities. The ketchup man said his name was Rashid Mahmoud Al Remidi, not Sean O'Toole as a partially burned draft card found among his sparse possessions seemed to indicate.

He said he might have been Sean O'Toole before he found himself, but he was more comfortable as Rashid. He said the Swami had released him from his former life of indigence, and being a new convert without a red sheet, he had doused himself with ketchup and pasta sauce in order to blend in with the group.

"Then how do you account for your race through town naked?" asked the Chief.

"In my haste, I grabbed some Tabasco sauce to finish off with, and it dribbled down on a very tender area. Believe me, that stuff is hot. I was in such agony that I just ran out and didn't get relief until I jumped into that watering trough out front," he explained.

If the events of that memorable evening didn't produce much, at least they put the town on the map—along with Berkeley and Woodstock.

# High Life in
# the Low Court

---

Low courts are called low courts because they don't enjoy a particularly high priority when it comes to space in the Town Hall. To get maximum usage out of a building that was built 175 years ago, when things were not as complex as they are today, the Court, which sits once or twice a week at most and then only at night, shares the use of the Selectmen's room with such disparate groups as the Budget Committee, the Ways and Means Committee, the Zoning Board of Adjustment, the Overseers of the Poor and the Cemetery Trustees sub-committee concerned about sunken graves, said to be an ongoing problem. Obviously, scheduling becomes an issue.

Occasionally the Budget Committee, which meets sporadically throughout the year, gets its dates mixed up and shows up on Court night, only to be relegated to the kitchen, where it may find itself conducting its deliberations under the baleful eye of a burglar the State Police have handcuffed to the stove for safekeeping pending his appearance before the court.

In the usual course of events, the Constable sets the stage by bellowing, "Dishonorable court now in session—all rise," as the Judge sweeps majestically into the room. Once the dust has settled, the Constable then assumes his functions as prosecutor and the show is on the road.

The Constable is apt to be a large, perspiring fellow, held together by a big Sam Brown belt, from which dangle a rusty gun, a pair of handcuffs and a can of Mace. Arranged in a row around the belt are a couple of dozen bullets polished to a high sheen. In fact they have been polished so often and for so long that they have worn thin, which accounts for the dribble of black powder every time the Constable hitches up his pants. Nothing else is polished—not the shoes, not the belt, not the gun—just the bullets. However, since the Constable is the only one charged with maintaining order in the courtroom, don't knock him, especially if you happen to be the Judge.

Actually, the Judge doesn't sweep in that majestically, having on previous occasions caught his gown on the fire extinguisher, setting it off and causing a cloud of white powder to fill the room. The same notoriously flamboyant judge once caught his judicial robes on a file cabinet and almost strangled when it fell over.

The preferred practice is to enter slowly and deliberately, with head slightly bowed under the weight of office, and then slam the record book on the table with a resounding whack, thereby dispelling any lingering notion you don't mean business.

Establishing the Court's authority early in the game is particularly important if sitting at the counsel table is the likes of Bruce MacTavish, Esq., from the lordly old-line firm of MacTavish, McGovern and M'God, a high-powered law mill from up in Manchester, who has been sent out by his father, Cyrus MacTavish, the hoary dean of the bar, to get a taste of the criminal side of things at the grassroots level.

Bruce, you will soon discover, is there to represent J. Percival Mortgagemoney, against whom a complaint has been lodged by his wife, Mary-Jane Mortgagemoney, alleging assault, in that he did come at her threatening to gouge her eyes out with a melon scoop, either while in his cups or in furtherance of some carnal purpose. The Constable drafted the complaint and is prosecuting, accounting for the latitude in the alleged motive.

"At approximately 2 a.m. on Thursday," the Constable intones, "I received a call advising me that Mr. Mortgagemoney, the bald-headed guy sitting over there, had just assaulted his wife, Mary

Jane, with a melon scoop. After donning my uniform with the badge prominently displayed, I proceeded to the Mortgagemoney residence, and upon my arrival, I found Mr. Mortgagemoney picking up broken dishes. Mrs. Mortgagemoney was located hiding in the broom closet, crying, with her hair all messed up and her bodice ripped asunder. I immediately arrested Mr. Mortgagemoney, and after questioning him extensively, I lodged this here complaint," he concludes triumphantly. Not quite the way the Attorney General of the City of New York would have handled it, but what you see is what you get in the local court.

Right about here Bruce MacTavish will arise, and after making a few silly remarks about his high regard for the court, which everyone discounts heavily, he will point out that absolutely everything the Constable has said is pure hearsay and inadmissible. To correct this inadvertent slip-up, the Constable will call Mary-Jane Mortgagemoney to the witness stand, presumably to testify against her husband.

However, the Judge cannot help but notice that Mrs. Mortgagemoney arose from a seat beside her husband. They had been holding hands, giving rise to the suspicion that maybe she isn't as all-fired mad at him now as she appeared to be a few days ago, during the melon scoop incident. This notion, while of no probative value whatsoever, is the key to what will follow, just as night follows day.

Mary-Jane will take the witness stand with obvious reluctance. This is not because she is a retiring type, because she's not. She's the program chairperson for the PTA, and that is no job for a butterfly. She's a real go-getter and everyone knows it. It will then come as no surprise that her testimony will be that of an utterly devoted wife and mother, that her husband is a devoted husband and father, that they both attend church regularly, he plays with the dogs and is a good provider. In fact, she will wonder out loud how anyone could have arrested her husband in the first place, just because he was being playful around the house, an observation that causes knowing snickers and whistles from the onlookers.

Bruce MacTavish, sensing victory in the air and not content to leave well enough alone, is apt to launch into a blistering cross-examination of the Constable, aimed at casting him in the guise of a villain for having invaded the sanctity of the home. The Constable will perspire profusely, and unless some measure of control is exercised by the Judge, the whole affair will become a complete shambles.

Control is exercised by interrupting the proceedings, suggesting, "It's getting a bit stuffy in here. I think I'll call a short recess. Counsel will please join me in chambers."

Chambers happens to be the kitchen of the Town Hall, where the Budget Committee is holding its deliberations in the company of the burglar. This is the point where the Judge can suggest to Bruce that if he'll stop bugging the poor Constable, there is a good possibility that the complaint against his client may be dismissed. The Constable will say that his lot is not a happy one, and that if Mary-Jane calls him again she'd better not expect a rapid response on the part of the police. Bruce will get in a last word to somehow further irritate the Constable, before retiring to confer with his client.

The next few minutes of the recess can be consumed listening to the burglar explain the effects of deficit financing to the Budget Committee, as the Constable samples the leftovers from the Library Trustee's coffee hour.

When Court reconvenes, Bruce MacTavish will ask leave of the Court to make a brief statement, and will explain that the parties have reconciled, rendering the present action mute. The Constable will mop his feverish brow and the burglar will take center stage.

Such is the business of the Low Court.

# Zeke Taggart
# and the Arsonist

There isn't much high crime around our neck of the woods, but when some does turn up it makes up for lost opportunities. Most of our criminal activity consists of a variety of misdemeanors and the occasional wife swapping, most of which goes undetected anyway. Being caught drunk while driving is characteristic of the most serious offenses that come to public attention.

Of course there's always an exception to the rule, and the matter of Zeke Taggart and the arsonist falls into this category. It really concerns Zeke, Officer Bergeron of the local constabulary, and the Deputy State Fire Marshal more than it does the arsonist, though he was the catalyst in the whole affair.

For a number of months the town suspected that an arsonist was on the loose. Six barns had mysteriously burned to the ground in a seemingly random series of unexplained fires. Barn fires are not uncommon around here, especially since dairying is no longer as lucrative as it once was, but six barns in two weeks? No way.

"Wal, I see lightnin' hit out at Philo Blivven's place. Didn't save nothin', did they?" was the usual comment each time another barn came to a smoky end.

"Better'n bankruptcy, if ya know what I mean," was a somewhat less charitable observation among the hard-pressed dairy farmers whose barns were still standing.

It wasn't long before the rash of fires attracted the attention of the State Fire Marshal. The local volunteer fire department looked upon these events as merely an opportunity to get in a few more drills before the town hall went up, and didn't even consider the possibility that an arsonist was loose in the community.

The State Fire Marshal, however, viewed the matter somewhat differently. He sent his best man into town under cover of an alias to get to the bottom of matter. However, the Marshal's best man was rather voluble, and it wasn t long before he was unmasked. Some said this was by design, because it enabled the Marshal to send in his *real* best man, Deputy State Fire Marshal Rufus Dinwiddie, who managed to remain incognito while he conducted his investigations, which certainly suggested arson. The presence of incendiary materials at each fire only served to confirm what everybody knew—the fires had a helper. The real problem was who he was, not where he would strike next. The opportunities for even a semi-skilled arsonist were legion.

In order to coordinate things, a top-secret meeting was held at the local police station, to which the Chief of Police invited only his best and most trusted officers, among them being Officer Bergeron, an eager beaver, who had a theory of his own on how to trap the arsonist. Nobody knows what was discussed at the meeting, but it is known that each and every barn in town was identified as a possible target, and there were more barns in town than most people thought there were. Quite a few of them were attached to older houses near the center of town, and though no longer used for their original purposes—many were devoted to an assortment of business and commercial undertakings—they were nevertheless inviting targets for the arsonist, especially if Officer Bergeron's theory was correct. There remained the game plan to give effect to what became known as The Bergeron Caper, and as is the custom in such situations, the chore of implementing the plan was given to the most ardent proponent. The scheme eventually worked, but it had untoward consequences.

According to Bergeron, much publicity should be given to establishing a barn watch on the more prominent outlying barns. A schedule of when the largest, most obvious targets were to be under surveillance should be published in the local newspaper. The schedule gave the locations of each of the barn watchers, with their tours of duty specified. Farm hands were publicly sworn to secrecy. With these barns so publicly and obviously covered, the theory went, it was unlikely that they would be targets for the arsonist's next strike.

Bergeron, in the meantime, embarked on the second aspect of his plan, namely that with the outlying barns so clearly and obviously covered, the arsonist would be inclined to strike at the less remote, in-town barns, which were easier to reach—and easier to cover.

To carry out this second and more technically demanding task, Bergeron enlisted a group of trusted officers, including Deputy State Fire Marshal Dinwiddie, to stake out the in-town barns. He surreptitiously took them on a tour of their assigned posts, suggesting that they mentally select a concealed vantage point from which to conduct their surveillances.

During the initial tour, the Deputy State Fire Marshal noticed a new pile of old shingles arranged in a pyramid over a wad of newspaper in the manure pit beneath Ezekiel Taggart's furniture storage barn. He pointed them out to Officer Bergeron.

Zeke, who conducted Zeke's Moving and Storage, used the barn to store his customers' furniture between their moves up the corporate ladder. Bergeron asked Zeke about the shingles, but the batteries in his hearing aid were low, so the conversation didn't amount to much.

Dinwiddie made a mental note of what he observed, and resolved to take up his position around Zeke's barn as a likely place for the arsonist to strike. A barn chock full of old bric-à-brac would certainly light off handsomely if it had a proper start.

"I'd like to take up my position at the Taggart barn," Dinwiddie said, adding, "That place would make a hell of a smudge, wouldn't it?" He neglected to mention the pile of shingles, which he regarded as highly suspicious.

Unbeknownst to anyone, Zeke had also noticed the pile of shingles in his old manure pit. Obviously this discovery gave the entire matter a sense of urgency only he appreciated. He had no confidence that the local police, or even the Deputy State Fire Marshal for that matter, had the slightest idea of what they were doing. He resolved to take matters in his own hands, which he did, telling nobody what he planned to do.

Unfortunately, Bergeron's plan did not include advising the owners of the various barns near town what the forces of law and order intended to do, nor when or how they planned to do it. This secretiveness only reinforced Zeke's determination to hack it on his own. He immediately set about developing his own scheme, which he hoped would protect him until the authorities got their act together.

Among the steps he took right away was the purchase of a new set of batteries for his hearing aid. He hadn't needed new ones for the past two years, and the enhanced power of the device, once the new batteries were installed, surprised him.

"Christ, now I can hear my wife," he said, with apparent displeasure.

Zeke then hit upon an even better use for the device. He recalled his service in WWII in an anti-aircraft battery, and the listening devices used before radar was invented to detect incoming planes. They consisted of large dishes, and a device that Zeke now assumed was a larger version of his hearing aid, centered in the dish.

To duplicate this arrangement, he took his wife's dishpan, placed it on edge on the railing of his back porch. He then Scotch-taped his hearing aid in the center of the pan, hooking it up to his earpiece with a couple of extension cords. With his hookup complete, Zeke took up his position just behind the kitchen door, with his shotgun on his lap. If as much as a leaf rustled, he was sure he'd hear it. If it turned out to be the arsonist, he was equally confident he could blow him away with both barrels.

About this same time Deputy State Fire Marshal Dinwiddie took up his position beneath Zeke's back porch. Double coverage prevailed; Zeke's hearing aid in his wife's dishpan with Zeke plugged into the other end, and the Deputy State Fire Marshal crouched beneath the same porch. Neither one knew of the presence of the other.

The precise details of subsequent events that memorable evening are a bit clouded, but the consensus seems to bear out that somewhere around 4 a.m. the Deputy State Fire Marshal heard a noise in the manure pit, prompting him to begin sneaking toward Zeke's barn.

Unfortunately, he caught his foot in the extension cord connecting Zeke with his hearing aid, pulling the pan off the railing and making one hell of a noise in Zeke's ear—awakening him with a start.

Zeke jumped up, grabbed his shotgun, and seeing a figure running across his back yard, let fly with both barrels. Fortunately his aim wasn't too good and all he did was blow the windshield out of his furniture van, parked beside the barn.

While all this was going on, Officer Bergeron, following his own game plan, was crouching over the manure hatch in the barn. He regarded his presence as an added measure of security, though he neglected to tell Dinwiddie that he would be there. It struck Officer Bergeron that a vantage point directly over the pile of shingles might be the best place from which to nail the arsonist. He could just jump down through the hatch right on top of the culprit, once he was sure of his man.

As luck would have it however, the arsonist, who had in fact targeted Zeke's barn, was understandably alarmed at Zeke's shotgun blasts and ran out of the manure stall just as Bergeron plunged down through the hatch above, missing the culprit entirely. The arsonist, being a quick thinker, grabbed the Deputy State Fire Marshal on the run, shouting, "Don't shoot, Zeke, I've got him," as he pinned the hapless Deputy State Fire Marshal's arms behind him.

While Zeke held Dinwiddie at bay with the shotgun, other officers, attracted by the commotion, rushed to the scene from their nearby posts and clapped handcuffs on Dinwiddie. Only after they had him back at the police station and identified did it dawn on them that the person who had been holding Dinwiddie was probably the arsonist, who by this time was long gone.

Fortunately, as Officer Bergeron plunged downward through the manure hatch, he recognized the arsonist—someone who had been rejected for membership in the fire department on the ground he was overqualified for the only position then available, that of strainerman on the suction hose section of Engine 2. All that remained was the apprehension of the culprit and the case could be closed.

The matter came to a head later that same night when the arsonist returned to Zeke Taggart's barn for the purpose of finishing the job he had only begun. What he didn't count on was that Officer Bergeron, applying his vast knowledge of the criminal mind at work, was again waiting over the manure hatch. As Bergeron hurtled down for the second time, this time successfully, the arsonist was heard to yell, "Jesus, not you again!"

The matter was concluded when the Deputy State Fire Marshal's case against Zeke Taggart, alleging assault with a deadly weapon, was dismissed on the ground of mistaken identity, an entirely novel defense in the annals of New Hampshire criminal law.

# Perambulating
## the Town Bounds

"51.2—Perambulation of Town Lines: The lines between the towns of this state shall be perambulated and the marks and bounds shall be renewed, once every seven years, forever, by the Selectmen of the Town or by such persons as they shall in writing appoint for the purpose." (Revised Statutes Annotated, 1942, of New Hampshire.)

So speaketh the law of New Hampshire, in consequence of which the Selectmen are supposed to walk the town bounds every seven years, so they won't get lost at other times.

When the palefaces first learned how to acquire land from the natives they found in residence when they got here—by just taking it—an Englishman by the name of Lord Jeffrey Amherst was running things from down Boston way. He had no idea of the size of the lands over which he had jurisdiction, other than that there was a lot of it, enough so that if someone of his acquaintance wanted a piece, he'd tell them to take their pick. Some say that Amherst, New Hampshire, came into being in this manner, and was named Amherst as a tribute to the great man's benevolence. There are others who say it is a testament to Lord Jeff's ability to dispense with dissidents.

The town's original settlers, wishing to eastablish their grant, began to set out granite markers in the woods, in order, as they said, "to nail down our corners." Others regarded this act as insurance against a change of attitude on the part of Lord Amherst. This practice inevitably led to some disagreement as to the outer reaches of their grant with adjacent beneficiaries of Lord Amherst's largess, all of whom sought to expand their own grants by simply adjusting their bounds from time to time.

After many years of this sort of carrying-on, disputes over where the boundaries actually were tended to be settled with muskets. To avoid depopulation of the countryside, the State was formed and said, in effect, "All right, enough of this nonsense. Let's settle this thing. Wherever the boundaries are right now, that's where they'll stay." There was a mad rush to find the location of the granite boundary markers, and thus was born the requirement that every seven years the Selectmen had to visit each and every marker to make sure they hadn't migrated again, to the advantage of a neighboring town.

Today Selectmen do not look forward to this task. It is one of the negative features of an otherwise ill-paying job. Fence Viewers, on the other hand, don't have periodically to walk the town fences; all they have to do is occasionally glance at a fence here and there to see if it conforms. What it conforms to is immaterial.

Nor do the Cemetery Trustees have very much to do to carry out their trust, because their charges aren't going anywhere anyway.

The committee organizing the 300th Anniversary of Amherst is apt to be rather lackadaisical too. All they do is meet now and then over cider and doughnuts in the kitchen of the town hall, where they scheme up vast plans. They're in no hurry, since the 300th anniversary is four years away.

Though the Selectmen were charged with inspecting the town bounds only every seven years, it was an annual undertaking. The town had several dozen granite markers strewn around in the woods, and the only practical way of visiting all of them within each seven-year cycle was to do a few of them each year. At the end of each seven-year cycle, they could say with a straight face that they had visited every one.

Because each boundary was not only a boundary marking the outer reaches of Amherst, it was also the same thing for the adjoining towns, and to avoid conflict in case of a disagreement, the Selectmen adopted the practice of contacting their counterparts in the adjoining towns to agree on a date for the perambulation. Any disagreement due to the unaccountable migration of a boundary could then be resolved on the spot.

At the crack of dawn on the appointed day, everyone would congregate in one town hall or the other, and pore over all the available maps, the most recent of which was apt to be a dry, brittle parchment, dated 1642. The conventional practice was then to retire to some convenient parlor, from which after the passage of a decent amount of time, a Certificate of Town Bounds materialized, all duly signed, sealed and delivered, attested to by everyone present, saying the town bounds were where they were supposed to be. To reinforce the probative weight of the certificate, casual visitors were drafted to further attest to the contents of the certificate.

This was particularly necessary in the case of the Amherst/Hollis bound, especially with respect to the northeast boundary common to both towns. The boys in Hollis were all right—it was the actual boundary stone that was the problem. In spite of a pile of certificates asserting its existence over the years, nobody had ever actually seen it. This lack never caused any problems and never interfered with the workings of either town. At least it didn't until Amherst elected a new Selectman—a newcomer to town and an overzealous, eager-beaver type, who worked for the Federal Government as an appraiser in the Department of Housing and Urban Development (HUD). This unsmiling and pristine fellow was shocked at the fraudulent conduct of previous Selectmen in not doing whatever was necessary actually to find the missing boundary stone once and for all.

"I'm totally shocked that you people would even think of certifying a bound without actually physically touching it," he intoned, adding, "This is tantamount to FRAUD!"

"Well, good for you, you malignant bastard," one of the assembled Selectmen said. "I guess we'll just have to appoint you a Committee of One to remedy this tremendous shortcoming, won't we?"

And they did. Everyone hoped this would so consume him for the balance of his term that he wouldn't have time to interfere in the normal course of business. A secret pact was entered by the Selectmen of both towns by the terms of which nobody would look for the recalcitrant if he happened to disappear in the course of his quest for the missing boundary stone.

"If he actually finds the damned thing, we'll have to account for it every seven years until we can manage to lose it again. Better we should lose him instead," they all agreed.

For several months the HUD fellow was strangely quiet. He didn't show up at his usual places and everyone thought he was busily engaged in his appointed task of finding the missing boundary stone. Actually he had hit upon a neat ploy whereby he too could shuffle off the legwork on someone else. He claimed he had found the missing bound but that it had fallen over, and being alone, he was unable to stand it upright. "Obviously," he said, "some vandals or rock hunters have uprooted it and it must be replaced." He said there had to be an official determination of the proper location, and slyly suggested that the judges of the municipal courts of the two towns be named an Impartial Committee of Two to reset it, and give their imprimatur of approval to the proper site. "Incidentally," he said, "they could paint it yellow so we can find it next time. The stone is already there."

Judge Banks of the neighboring town was a man of many moons and had no more intention of wandering around in the underbrush than did Judge Lincoln of our town. Neither of them really cared very much one way or the other whether the boundary stone was actually located or that it be painted yellow, but they couldn't shirk their duty.

"We ought to be able," Judge Banks observed to Judge Lincoln, "to outsmart that slippery bastard at his own game, don't you think?"

"If we can't, we'd better pack it in," said Judge Lincoln, a man known for his penetrating legal opinions.

What follows is the very first revelation of what happened to the Amherst/Hollis town bound, as recalled by one who ought to know.

At a cost of $35.00 paid for out of the fines collected by the two courts, they hired a small plane at the nearby Nashua airport, and had themselves flown over the general area on a sort of preliminary reconnaissance mission, to locate, if they could, some easy means of getting to the most likely spot where the missing boundary stone was supposed to be without the need to blaze their own trail. They were both surprised and overjoyed to discover that if their plots were correct, the general area where the bound ought to be was pretty generally a vast swamp, impassable to all but the lowest forms of life.

"No wonder nobody ever actually found the blame thing," observed Judge Banks. "It was probably never set out in the first place. Obviously, God never intended that a boundary stone be set there, nor is one going to be set there now, especially if you and I have to do it," he concluded.

"But what do you suppose that story about finding it tipped over was intended to accomplish?" asked Judge Lincoln.

"It was nothing more than an artful dodge, calculated to make someone else find the spot and actually set the stone," said Judge Banks.

Their further analysis revealed that if the actual site was an impassable swamp and if no boundary stone had ever been set, none could have been found a half mile away, or anywhere else, for that matter. The whole story was a complete fabrication designed to conceal the fact that the HUD fellow had encountered the swamp, all of which he correctly perceived as a deliberate attempt to do away with him. The two judges, having used up only half of their $35.00 plane ride, elected to continue their flight to get their money's worth.

Upon their return, they got out the old maps and found they were not all that bad. They contained courses and distances and the like, though they neglected to mention the swamp. A new map was created in a most professional style, along with a voluminous report to the Selectmen of both towns, indicating that the precise location of the missing bound had been determined. All that remained was to paint it bright yellow in order that it might be more easily located in future years. For the convenience of later generations, the spot was off a continuation of the old Aaron Stewart Road, best accessed from the Hollis end. Nothing was said about getting to it from the Amherst end, because it was under several feet of swamp water. The report concluded that the HUD man should now feel perfectly free to undertake the marking of the boundary.

The report, as presented to the Selectmen of both towns, was immediately approved as submitted. The HUD fellow was directed to undertake painting the stone because he was the newest man on the board, and it would be he who would have to direct future Selectmen to the site, because everyone presently on the Board would be gone before the thing had to be located again. It would save a lot of time and effort if one of the remaining men knew where it could be located.

There is no sequel to this tale, because the records are barren on what subsequently transpired. About three weeks later, the HUD Selectman resigned, saying he had taken a position with IBM in New York. Passed papers on his house the following month.

History has a way of repeating itself.

# Sex in the Organ Loft

It is no great secret that sex goes on pretty much all over the place. In fact many of our most devout and puritanical ancestors, after they figured it out, practiced it religiously and with evangelical fervor. Though the resulting large families were attributed to that most Christian of virtues, love, there was always the lingering suspicion that the process caught on for more earthy reasons. Given this auspicious sponsorship, it is no wonder the local village church was the scene of one of its more bizarre manifestations.

It all began when a newcomer to town, a bachelor mechanical engineer by trade, plunged right into local affairs by joining the Congregational Church. And it wasn't long before he convinced the vestrymen that the venerable old organ Miss Fraggle, the elderly organist, abused every Sunday morning was in dire need of his professional attention.

"Why, that organ leaks air all over the place, and it's amazing that it's still served by a manual air pump. Between the leaks and erratic pumping by volunteers, it's a wonder it works at all," he said, adding, "That organ should be served by an electric compressor with a large air reservoir; then and only then will it achieve its full potential."

Naturally, the mechanical engineer cum organ specialist was just the man for the job. The vestry unanimously appointed him a Committee of One to accomplish the renovation.

The organ in question was state of the art in its heyday about the year 1850. It was a genuine pipe organ, brought to life every Sunday morning by the Herculean efforts of pairs of elderly vestrymen, who alternated as pump men. This meant that they had to work the hand pump that supplied air to the pipes, so that Miss Fraggle, a spinster during the week but church organist on Sunday, could release it indiscriminately as she randomly but vigorously pounded the keys, especially when she was into Onward Christian Soldiers and Faith of Our Fathers, two of her favorites.

Miss Fraggle liked to lay it on the base pipes, which rattled the windows and consumed vast quantities of air. If she happened to get carried away with her efforts, the pump men were apt to get exhausted trying to keep up with her demands—for air, that is. They were always threatening to resign unless she modified her technique, and they welcomed the idea that the air pump could be converted to electric power. "Only way to go!" they chorused.

There was, as a consequence, a small but influential element who, though certainly out of character if it involved spending money, nevertheless supported the entire idea. Their only other hope was that Miss Fraggle might become a Catholic, and her successor be somewhat less demanding.

After a detailed survey in the spring, the mechanical engineer began his work during the summer months, when church attendance habitually took a back seat to more leisurely pursuits. Aside from a month's delay while the vestry arranged to have the church electrical system upgraded, to supply the 220-volt current the new pump required, nobody paid much attention to what the mechanical engineer was doing—until late in August, when he discovered that the reinvigorated air supply so unnerved the ancient organ pipes that retuning them was necessary.

But the mechanical engineer needed a set of special tuning forks to obtain the precise pitch characteristic of the truly professional job he said he could do. Unfortunately, the church lacked anything that came anywhere near matching the pipes of the old organ. Somehow this shortfall had to be corrected or everything would be for naught.

Being a dedicated parishioner, the mechanical engineer had noted that a Comely Young Thing in the choir had sufficient range to duplicate most of the pipe notes. He suggested that she might be willing to volunteer in place of the tuning forks.

Unfortunately she was the only daughter of a local cow farmer, and she was needed on the farm to cook and do housework, limiting her availability to evenings after the dishes were done. This was OK with the mechanical engineer, because he was contributing his time and effort anyway, and about all the spare time he had was at night after his regular work.

When fall arrived and church attendance began to pick up, the organ received wide acclaim. Delegations from surrounding towns came to hear Miss Fraggle achieve her thundering crescendos playing such hymns as Amazing Grace and The Battle Hymn of the Republic. Though there was general agreement that the old organ had begun a new life, the mechanical engineer was still not satisfied.

"I still have a few errant pipes," he said, "but with a little more work, I'm sure I can get every single pipe properly adjusted." Most people thought that, compared to what they had been, things were in pretty good shape. However, the mechanical engineer insisted on achieving perfection, and continued to work on those few errant pipes. The Comely Young Thing continued to contribute her clear, bell-like voice evenings after the chores were done, even though Miss Fraggle thought the organ was perfectly tuned as it was.

"Don't see why it needs more tuning," she said, "it sounds fine to me."

It was only because Miss Fraggle thought the old organ was in tune even before the restoration that her views were discounted. This attitude was further reinforced by the obvious, ongoing efforts of the mechanical engineer and the Comely Young Thing, when her clear, bell-like voice could be heard echoing through the empty church hall late at night. Passing neighbors thought the passionate sound was attributable to the dedication of the Comely Young Thing and the mechanical engineer—which it was.

Late in the fall the mechanical engineer declared his work complete. A ceremony was planned to honor him and the Comely

Young Thing, for "their dedication to organs," the program said—a prescient observation, as it turned out. It was only after the wedding, performed in the church a month in advance of the birth of their first child, that the full scope of their joint efforts was fully appreciated by the congregation.

Miss Fraggle said they should name their firstborn Double Bass, because the only place there was room enough was beneath the bass chamber.

The vestry wondered how she knew.

# Dog Damage and
# the King's Daughters

Clem Witherspoon has the distinction of owning the only two-town henhouse in the entire state. It's a double-decker affair that sits astride the Milford/Amherst town line. The north half is in Amherst and the south half is in Milford.

When Clem was in his prime, and before the business moved South, Clem used to raise 25,000 broilers at a shot. After he turned 75, he still kept his hand in by raising a modest 5,000 birds, which he distributed equally between the first and second floors of his henhouse.

"A man cain't lay around on his dead ass just because he's 75," Clem said. "Anyway, it helps with my taxes to have a few birds to sell around town."

Then disaster struck. During the dark of one night last spring, something so unnerved the hens on the first floor of the Amherst end of the henhouse that they all flocked to the Milford end, where they piled up and suffocated.

The tumult caused by this event, occurring as it did at the Milford end, alarmed the hens on the floor above, and in their efforts to escape, they flocked to the opposite, or Amherst, end of the second floor, where they duplicated the carnage that had occurred on the first floor.

No matter how Clem looked at it, he had about 2,000 dead hens on his hands, divided into two piles, one in Milford and the other in the Amherst. The question in Clem's mind was how he could salvage something from this catastrophe. It was then that the light dawned.

New Hampshire has an old statute that makes towns responsible for damage done by dogs when their owners are unknown. This sort of law was necessary years ago when the principal activity around here was sheep farming, and dogs running loose wreaked havoc with the flocks.

"Hattie," Clem said to his wife, "if'n it was dogs what scair't our hens, then maybe this here old law will let us put in a claim to both towns for the birds that died in each one," he reasoned, adding, "You call the fellow that runs the mink farm down in Greenville. He'll cart em off to feed to his mink. This is Selectmen's meetin' day in both towns and I'll be too busy filin' our claim to lug the dead'uns to the dump."

Hattie wasn't too enthusiastic about assuming responsibility for the dead birds, because she was the hostess for the King's Daughters, who were meeting at the house that very day to begin making aprons to sell at the annual church fair, and she had to bake some teacakes to keep the ladies' strength up for that event.

"Oh, Clem, you always leave me with these problems. But maybe the ladies will want to pluck a few, so we can all have some for the freezer."

Clem set about laying out his claim for dog damages. He first approached the Milford Selectmen, who summarily rejected the claim.

"Clem, whatever got them birds all het up, did it in Amherst. The fact that they flocked to our end to die is immaterial. It's where the *mense rea* occurred that counts," said the First Selectman, proud of the fact that he knew what *mense rea* meant, even if nobody else did. "You'd better file your claim in Amherst," he said.

Clem, faced with that setback, then went to the Amherst Selectmen and sought to convince them they should pay.

"Clem, your second floor hens may have died in Amherst, but the thing that got them going was the tumult on the first-floor

Milford end of your hen house. You'd better file in Milford, because we won't pay for something that started in Milford."

Having been turned down by Milford, Clem felt Amherst was his
only source of recompense, and he pushed it all he could.

"You boys have it all wrong. It's like to that fellow that got shot
last year. He was shot in New Hampshire, but he crawled over
the line into Massachusetts, where the benefits are better. Where
did the crime occur? In New Hampshire, where he was shot, or
Massachusetts, where he died?" he asked. "I got the same thing,
only with hens," he asserted, convinced that the Selectmen would
see the logic of his position, but they didn't.

However, Clem Witherspoon was not exactly an untutored nun
in a house of ill-repute when it came to dealing with selectmen.
He figured if he kept at it long enough, he'd find a way around
their arguments. On his way back to see the Milford Selectmen
again, an idea came to him.

"You fellows have this all wrong. Your *mense rea* didn't begin in
Amherst, it began in Milford, where the hens first piled up and
died. That was both the site of the first difficulty and it caused the
problem on the second floor. No matter how you look at it,
Milford is responsible," he said, with assurance.

"I see your point, Clem," said Milford's First Selectman, adding,
"but how do you know dogs caused the whole thing? Maybe it
was a fox, or a skunk, or something. If it was, they aren't covered
by the statute on dog damage, so you're out of luck either way."

That night, when he arrived home from a pretty discouraging day, he reported his doings to Hattie.

"I guess we've just got to swallow our loss," he said, "because I cain't get nowhere with neither town. 'Stead of givin' those birds to the mink fella, we should'a tried to sell 'em for somethin'. If he paid anything at all, we'd be ahead of where we are now."

"Oh, don't worry, Clem," Hattie said. "When I told the King's Daughters about it, they all agreed to pitch in an we plucked the entire lot. Then Maude Tillinghast got her son—the County Commissioner, you know—on the phone and he agreed to take the whole lot for the the Old Folk's Home if the price was right. Said the old folks were gettin' a bit militant about the food lately, and a run of chicken dinners would be a cheap solution to that problem."

"Gawd, Hattie, that was great. But what price did he agree to pay?"

"The King's Daughters figured that if the county didn't have to pluck the birds, they should pay a premium price. We settled on thirty-seven cents a pound, delivered. That's where we been—deliverin' the birds," she said.

Clem began to see the wisdom of having married Hattie in the first place. For years it was a toss-up, but now he was sure his judgment 52 years ago was sound.

"Hattie, that's more than they'd brought if we'd sold 'em to the chicken-plucking plant. What's the catch?" he asked, always hedging his bets.

"Well, we King's Daughters figure our services are worth a dime a pound, so you owe us $174.10," she said. "With that kind of money we won't have to make so many of those darned fancy aprons to sell at the fair."

Clem thought it over for a few minutes. "You girls drive a hard bargain,' he said, "but I guess I'll have to go along with it."

"Don't you complain, Clem," Hattie observed. "Before we decided to do the job ourselves we got a price from the D.A.R., but they wanted fifteen cents a pound."

# The Village Bird
# Watchers' Society
# vs the Town Fire Horn

One of the more enduring features of most New England towns is their continuing reliance on the services of volunteer fire departments. Historically these aggregations began as bucket brigades in Colonial times. Every able-bodied citizen had his own leather bucket, and whenever the cry "FIRE!" was heard, they'd all grab their buckets and run for the nearest well, to begin passing buckets of water toward the fire until whatever was burning was finally consumed by flames.

As time went on, and the basic inadequacy of the bucket routine dawned on everyone, sophisticated equipment emerged, like hand-tubs, which had to be stored in some central location. Instead of each volunteer bringing his own bucket, the new routine called for summoning the volunteers to wherever the hand-tub was stored. When a sufficient number of men had gathered, they'd manhandle the tub to a source of water and begin pumping up and down on the handles to get water to the fire.

As towns grew, hand-tub companies multiplied, giving rise to some rather spectacular clashes, as the companies vied to be the first to arrive at a fire. These encounters frequently resulted in brawls that occupied the contestants until the burning building was reduced to ashes.

As time went on and motorized equipment was developed, the old hand-tub companies embraced the new technology with a vengeance. Fire companies became somewhat more structured, though even today they still rely on volunteers for manpower. They now summon the troops by means of a fire horn, which can be heard all over town.

Nobody in his right mind ever votes against the firemen, and when they say the want a new fire horn, they get a new fire horn. This has resulted in many microscopic towns having fire horns that echo among the hills, as though announcing the Second Coming.

Over the years, these horns have developed a high state of efficiency. They are now generally air powered, and rival the county-wide alarm system designed to alert the entire state if the Seabrook nuke plant ever lights off. Their ability to rattle windows all over town is legendary.

"Ya gotta be able to hear it, wherever yer at," the firemen say, when some elderly widow complains that the last time the horn went off her canary fell off its perch and hasn't been the same since, or the parson prays the sound won't shatter the only remaining stained-glass window in the church, which somehow managed to survive the Great Church Fire of 1823, even though the church itself didn't.

This persistent horn problem and its most recent ramifications are the subject of this treatise.

For years it had been the practice of the Amherst fire department to test their fire horn on Saturday by sounding the "all clear, return to station" signal at noon. Of course they also blew it to announce drill night, monthly during the winter and weekly during the summer, along with the "no school" signal, among others.

In short, the fire horn had plenty of exercise, quite apart from alerting the firemen that something was afire, an event for which it was allowed to blow until its air supply was exhausted. The old-timers, recognizing that early alert of the firemen was preferable to seeing their barns go up in smoke and flames, put up with the ear-splitting blasts as the price they had to pay for the benefits of civilization. The horn also provided a break in what some thought of as a pretty dull existence anyway.

As the town grew, much to the dismay of the old-timers, new people moved in, paying exorbitant prices for the stately homes around the village green. The ear-shattering blasts of the fire horn gradually became an issue with these types, especially if it went off just as they sat down to make their monthly mortgage payment, or enjoy a pitcher of 'tini's beside their backyard barbecue.

"Good God, is that the nuke plant going up, or is it just a brush fire?" people were likely to ask whenever the horn sounded. Once when somebody saw flames in Ted Transistor's back yard, and blew the "in town" signal, the entire department turned out, and charged right into an informal meeting Ted was conducting to indoctrinate his new recruits in the sales department.

By the time the vamps realized that the fire was nothing more than an open barbecue pit, and managed to shut down their two and a half inch line (the beer drinkers had extinguished the fire themselves in time-honored fashion), Ted's back yard looked like low tide on the clam flats. All his wicker lawn furniture was washed up against the side of his garage, such was the water pressure in the compact part of town.

Events of this sort kept the fire-horn issue alive, but what really brought the matter to a head was the indignation it generated among the members of the Village Bird Watchers' Society, the day the horn gave out one of its notorious blasts just as they were passing the fire house one Saturday morning, while on an in-town spotting bee.

It wasn't really the noise that got them all wrought up, it was the pigeons. During an uncharacteristic lull in fire-horn activity, a family of pigeons had selected the bass horn as a nice spot to build a nest and start their family.

Startled by the blast of the horn, the birders looked up just in time to see the entire pigeon family, young and old alike, blown right out the mouth of the horn. To suggest they were indignant as they watched the feathers float gently to earth is an understatement—they were positively LIVID!

"Oh, the cruelty of at all!" they said in chorus. "We'll simply have to do something to prevent this sort of thing happening again!" They immediately retired to the kitchen of one of their members to consider what sort of action to take.

It took them some time to get organized, but once they did, things really began to happen. One of their number was a retired lawyer, an expert in securities and leveraged buyouts, who volunteered his legal expertise to mastermind the project. He was thought to be well-qualified for the job, having spent a good part of his professional career defending arbitrageurs and junk-bond dealers on Wall Street, though his grassroots legal experience was somewhat more limited.

Other members, schooled in environmental concerns and having nothing better to do, busied themselves attacking the Town Dump from time to time as an environmental travesty that should be closed. With these overwhelming qualifications to bring to bear on the problem, the Birders soon devised a plan of attack.

Their first shot was across the bow of the town Selectmen, to protest the "wanton destruction of our wild life," an attack which the Selectmen sought to deflect by suggesting that the pigeons were "pests anyway, so what's all the fuss about?"

"Their droppings are all over General Grant's statue on the village green, and it takes the highway department all day to clean up just before Memorial Day," the Selectmen said.

Having gotten nowhere with the Selectmen, the Birders hunkered down for the long pull.

They next contacted something called The New England Pigeon Society on the theory that these worthies would immediately jump in and lend their support. Much to their dismay, the New England Pigeon Society shied away from doing anything concrete, saying, "We're primarily concerned with carrier pigeons, and we try to avoid all contact with the wild variety," implying that the wild variety were responsible for carrier pigeon rape. They did however, encourage our Birders to take local action, which the locals had already tried and found singularly ineffective.

The Selectmen, in the meantime, were somewhat surprised by the apparently benign response of the Birders, which they mistakenly attributed to the Birders' belated recognition of what the wild pigeons had been doing to General Grant's statue—until the writ was served, directing the Selectmen to "show cause, if any you have, why the relief prayed for in the within petition for injunction should not be granted."

The relief prayed for was the temporary and permanent cessation of blowing of the subject horn by the defendants, their agents and servants. The writ was turned over to Town Counsel with the admonition to "take this thing and do your professional best with it; that is, lose it somewhere. You've always been pretty good at that."

Town Counsel said, "You just leave it to me. I'm sure this whole affair will peter out, and even if it doesn't, we can procrastinate enough, with the vast store of dilatory tactics so dear to the hearts and minds of all lawyers, that nothing will happen until you're all out of office."

Unfortunately, both the Selectmen and Town Counsel misjudged the determination of the Birders, a fact that abruptly came to their attention by way of a Bill of Interpleader filed by something calling itself The Environmental Advocacy League, a process by which the League sought to enter the fray on the side of the Birders.

Shortly thereafter, an *Amicus Curiae* (Friend of the Court) brief arrived, adding another seemingly unrelated group to the affair. *Amicus Curiae* briefs are generally used when some clutch of busybodies decides to insert themselves into someone else's lawsuit, which they do by becoming Friends of the Court.

No court in its right mind ever welcomes them as friends, or anything else for that matter, regarding them more or less as so much legal flotsam and jetsam, which obscure the real issues.

The local Birders enlisted the support of this group, which maintained an office in Concord, the state capital, a fact that could not be ignored. The moralists were coming out of the woodwork.

Town Counsel had dealt with this sort of thing, though not on the scale that seemed to be unfolding. Nevertheless, he reassured the Selectmen, saying, "I'll file a few motions to buy us some time; that always works." This activity, in addition, enabled him to keep the legal meter running, a condition said to be hereditary among lawyers.

Counsel for the Birders, himself an avid bird watcher, as well as fancying himself an accomplished pleader of obscure legal causes, filed a motion for discovery, intended to discover what the town was up to. He neglected to mention just what it was he wanted to discover, a fact Town Counsel regarded as a fatal flaw, and concerning which Town Counsel intended to educate the Birder's Counsel, though not all at once.

"The case is in cruise control, let it coast," he said to the Selectmen. "I'll just suck him in a bit and then spring the trap. This bird guy apparently isn't aware of that ancient Doctrine of Sovereign Immunity, which says you can't sue the Sovereign. Since the town is the Sovereign in this situation, it can't be sued."

The Selectmen thought Town Counsel spoke with unaccustomed conviction, especially if by asserting this position, he minimized his chances of garnering an appropriate fee.

"Christ, if you picture us as medieval monarchs, said the First Selectman, "we'll never win, or even get re-elected for that matter. Can't you come up with something less intimidating? After all, the Birders vote too, you know."

"Oh, don't worry about that," Town Counsel reassured them. "The Doctrine of Sovereign Immunity just says that they can't sue you unless you consent. If the Democrats seem to be gaining strength from this, you can always consent, you know."

Though a detailed expose of the various legal ploys subsequently advanced by the parties might be interesting to those who get their highs from contemplating such things as the local implications of the GATT Treaty, a full revelation of such monkeyshines would make for some pretty boring reading. Suffice it to say that only a couple of them deserve consideration. All the others do nothing whatsoever to advance the cause, other than to reveal why lawyers cost so much and why they are in such bad repute.

The Selectmen, being a cow farmer, a retired insurance adjuster and a backhoe operator, respectively, directed Town Counsel to cut out all this crap and get this thing shut down, because the budget item for legal fees and canine injury went up the flue when Mattie Richard's dog took a hunk out of the census taker last fall.

Realizing the finite nature of the funds available to support his services lent a sense of urgency to the efforts of Town Counsel, causing him to hit the books, usually a completely foreign undertaking for him. He was amazed at the gold mine of useful information his research uncovered.

For example, he learned that while the Town owned the fire trucks, actual title to the firehouse and its trappings, including the subject fire horn, belonged to something called The Lawrence Hand-Tub Company, a charitable corporation established in 1817.

This clearly placed ownership of the horn in the hand-tub company, which would enable it to take advantage of another anomaly of the law—charitable immunity—thereby isolating it from the suit too. But the hand-tub company hadn't been sued yet, because the Birder's lawyer hadn't done his homework either.

It was equally apparent that the town itself had no official municipal fire department, this function having been assumed by the Lawrence Hand-Tub Company years ago, and never relinquished. The present-day fire department is simply a manifestation of the original 1817 volunteer organization. The fact that the town supplied the members with fire trucks instead of buckets only served to keep the group interested, and avoided the need to hire a professional crew.

It also meant that in suing the town, the Birders had sued the wrong party. The town didn't own the fire horn at all.

But being mindful that the source of fees to sustain and exploit the developing situation was finite, Town Counsel grabbed the bull by the horns and filed two motions, one raising the defense of Sovereign Immunity, and the other the defense of "You've sued the wrong party anyway." Town Counsel then awaited developments, having in mind that if the hand-tub company were sued, he had a good chance of obtaining another client to bill.

The Birders, having discovered the flaw in their case, moved to amend their petition by joining the Lawrence Hand-Tub Company as a party defendant, but the Court disallowed the motion, saying that in the absence of personal service on the hand-tub company, the court has no jurisdiction. "You can't just run around joining people as defendants without at least serving them with a copy of the complaint," the Judge ruled, thereby suggesting to the Birders lawyer what he had to do—which he then did.

Unfortunately, the sheriff served the papers on the only employee of the Lawrence Hand-Tub Company he could find, one Ezekiel Tibbetts, an aging vamp beyond his prime, whose sole function was to fire up the coffee urn in the firehouse every time an alarm sounded. He was not now a member of the company, however.

He had been a member for 69 years before being forced to assume emeritus status due to his waning ability to stand up for very long. He was also the custodian of the Boston Globe Cane, traditionally handed down to the oldest live resident of town, and passed along to his successor when he no longer had a use for it, an event that in Ezekiel's case hadn't yet arrived.

Once again Town Counsel filed a motion, only this time on behalf of the Lawrence Hand-Tub Company, pleading improper and ineffectual service in that the person served with process is not a member of the within named charitable defendant, thereby raising still another obstacle to the Birder's case. He was confident that the hand-tub treasury would support his preliminary ploy, though it might mean the supply of beer at the annual Firemen's Muster was a tad tight.

Counsel for the Birders was beside himself with frustration for having overlooked a fundamental precept of all litigation—it takes two to tango. He was further upset by the Judge's observation, "Don't you think it's about time you people consider the possibility of settlement? I'm due to retire next year and I don't want something like this case hanging over my head just as my years of putting up with this sort of thing are about to pay off."

Town Counsel, being mindful of the paucity of funds available to support lengthy litigation, nodded knowingly at the Judge's suggestion and offered to take it up with his client.

The matter was finally rendered mute, a term lawyers use to describe a situation in which the prospect of meaningful fees has vanished. The hand-tub company was persuaded to place a screen over the mouth of the horn, thereby rendering it unattractive to pigeon homesteading. They reckoned it was cheaper to do that than pay to win in court.

It is hoped the entire episode contains some germ of contemporary value, though it may only reveal the inner workings of the legal mind when it is unable to see the forest for the trees.

# Politics

Local politics really don't amount to very much when compared with the regional and national brouhahas that arise every two to four years. However, occasionally, when a contest is thought to represent the traditional division in which newcomers seek to displace the old-timers who have been running the place for the past decade or so, things begin to heat up a bit.

There are a few races in which a couple of people with absolutely nothing else to do run for such offices as Fence Viewer or Cemetery Trustee, but by and large these don't involve much acrimonious bickering. A candidate for Fence Viewer might float a rumor that he is better qualified because his glasses are thicker, but aside from that, nothing much happens.

The important offices, such as Selectman, are much more apt to bring out the aggressive tendencies in everyone even remotely involved. The usual confrontation is between a long-time resident who has been a Selectman for a number of years, and a relative newcomer to town, who acts as though he is appalled at how the town has been mismanaged in the past, saying that he is running just to bring some order to this chaos.

Aside from a few coffee hours put on by a candidate's wife, to which everyone is invited but only her immediate friends attend, the campaigns are pretty much characterized by public announcements that appear periodically in the local press, an example of which follows:

NOTICE

I hereby declare that I am a candidate for the office of Selectman of the Town of Amherst. I welcome the support of all the citizens concerned about the enforcement of zoning, adequate schools and fair assessments.

(Signed)
Ted Transistor

An excerpt from the February 15th issue of the same local paper, in response to the immediately preceding notice:

### NOTICE

I hereby advise all my friends and acquaintances that I plan to stand for re-election for another three-year term as Selectman of Amherst. I am confident that my faithful service over the past nine years as your Selectman have given me the wisdom and experience for the challenges ahead.

(Signed)
Percy Whipple
Born in Amherst

Excerpt from the February 23rd issue of the same local paper:

### SOCIAL NOTE

Fleepsie Snapser of Bloody Brook Run will hold a coffee hour for candidate for Selectman Ted Transistor, hardworking husband of our PTA president, Betty (Newmother) Transistor. 10 a.m. Friday, BYOB.

Item from the March 7th issue of the same paper:

> The last official meeting of
> the Board of Selectmen was
> held at the town hall last
> evening. All three selectmen
> were in attendance. The Board
> unanimously extended its ap-
> preciation to Percy Whipple,
> whose term expires at town
> meeting next week, for the
> fine effort he has shown over
> the past nine years, especially
> during this assessment year. It
> is hoped that Percy's succes-
> sor, if it isn't Percy, will ap-
> proach the task of assessing
> with the same devotion and
> fairness Percy has shown over
> the years. The meeting closed
> with a vote of no confidence
> in our Viet Nam policy.

The following quotation is from a political flier found in all the
mailboxes in town, addressed to "Boxholder, Amherst, N.H.":

"The following groups have endorsed the candidacy of Ted
Transistor of Mack Hill Road, who is running for Selectman:
The PTA, The Men's Tennis Association, The Electronic
Engineers Club, The Ham Radio League of Amherst, Citizens
for a Better Amherst, Individuals too numerous to mention."

This was about the sum total of political activity around town
until election day, when Percy Whipple parked his pickup truck
across from the town hall. On the back of the truck was a poster
that read as follows:

```
┌─────────────────────────────────────────────────────────┐
│                                                         │
│           PERCY WHIPPLE FOR SELECTMAN                   │
│                                                         │
│    I've lived here longer, and I've paid more          │
│        taxes than anyone else in town.                 │
│                                                         │
│              I HAVE EXPERIENCE                          │
│                                                         │
│        VOTE FOR WHIPPLE—GET EXPERIENCE                  │
│                                                         │
└─────────────────────────────────────────────────────────┘
```

On March 9th, the day after the election, the local newspaper
published the results:

> The Moderator announced hat
> the results of the recent election
> for Selectman in Amherst were
> as follows:
> Percy Whipple (incumbent) 687
> Ted Transistor                93
> Mother Theresa (write-in)      3

# The Exorcism Exercise

The business of running a small New England town is not exactly a bowl of cherries. Things that wouldn't cause a ripple anywhere else attain monumental proportions in New England, given the finely tuned sensitivities of the local population. For example, the running argument between the King's Daughters and the D.A.R. over priority in the use of the community tea service, which the King's Daughters were instrumental in obtaining for the use of the town, may never end.

The Historical Society wants to use it for its annual open house, but that event coincides with the regularly scheduled meeting of the King's Daughters, who claim precedence because it was their initial fund-raising efforts that bought it. Somehow these problems get resolved; the more bizarre ones cause the real difficulties.

One such event was the discovery of an uncharted burial vault outside the granite wall that surrounds Old Town Cemetery. It came to light when the Road Agent felt the ground suddenly give way beneath his truck, as he backed up to the wall to drop off a load of topsoil he was going to use to level off a number of sunken gravesites that have wilted over the years. Upon climbing out of his truck, he discovered that the entire rear end was down in what he at first thought was a subterranean washout.

It was only after he had extricated his truck with the aid of the town bucket loader that he discovered the weight of the truck and its load had collapsed the granite roof of an uncharted chamber of some sort. Since it was outside the cemetery wall, it never occurred to him that it might be a long-forgotten and unrecorded burial vault. Nor did it occur to him that it might also be occupied, a fact he confirmed once he had extricated his truck. The chamber held what was left of three caskets and their contents.

The Road Agent decided right on the spot that the best course of action was just to get hold of some granite slabs, repair the roof of the vault, and let it go at that. The occupants of the chamber weren't going anywhere, so why stir up a rumpus that he was sure would occur if he did anything else? Anyway, the thing was in the road right-of-way, so it fell within his official responsibility.

In furtherance of this plan, he sent the loader off to the Town Barn to pick up a couple of old granite slabs left over from the repair job on the Col. Wilkins Road bridge, which the State Game Warden had blown to pieces the previous summer.

The job proved to be somewhat more complex than he had originally estimated. The old broken slabs had to be removed, the new slabs lowered into place, and the whole thing graded over. This took two days, during which the entire scene was exposed to public view, during which it came to the attention of Father Sean O'Toole, the pastor of the Catholic Church in nearby Milford.

Father O'Toole seldom had occasion to invade the provinces of Rev. Clarence Potter, the pastor of the local Congregational Church, but one of his infrequent calls to preside over a burial in New Town Cemetery occurred while the chamber was being repaired. Being a conscientious cleric, he volunteered to conduct appropriate ceremonies to, as he said, "reconsecrate these hallowed grounds."

"You can do it if you like, Father, but how do you know these people planted in this here hole were Catholics?" asked the Road Agent. "Maybe they were Unitarians, in which case you'd be wastin' your time."

"I'll look up the records, and if there are none, I can handle the job on the basis of reclaiming lost souls," Father O'Toole said.

The following day Father O'Toole appeared at the Town Hall to consult the old records of burials in Old Town Cemetery, only to discover that they were maintained by the Rev. Potter, presumably because he did most of the business at both cemeteries, but really because he was Chairman of the Cemetery Trustees, an official town body. The records were in Potter's study in the Congregational Church. Father O'Toole made an appointment with the Rev. Potter to review the records on the basis of professional courtesy.

It didn't take the two clerics long to discover that no precise knowledge of the occupants of the chamber existed. It had been the practice in the distant past to prohibit the burial of witches and others possessed of the devil in Old Town Cemetery, most of whose occupants were not thought to be in that category.

Since the collapsed vault was just outside the cemetery wall, they concluded that the occupants of the chamber were buried there in deference to the class distinctions enjoyed by those residing on the other side of the wall, thereby placing those in the outside chamber under the general jurisdiction of Father O'Toole. He then proposed that he conduct an exorcism as part of the proceedings.

"I have more experience in this sort of thing than you do, Clarence," he said.

"Oh, I don't know about that, Sean; I have several of your people in my congregation, you know," the Rev. Potter observed, and intending to sink the spear a bit deeper, he said, "furthermore, Old Town Cemetery is my beat and I won't play second fiddle to you as long as you won't let me operate in your cemetery over in Milford," thereby rekindling a running dispute between them.

"Clarence, you know I'd let you perform for my audiences, only I have a jurisdictional problem to contend with. I'd have to get the permission of the Bishop, and he'd have to get the O.K. from the Pope, and by that time the whole thing would be a dead issue— no pun intended. Instead, why don't we run a double-header? You preach the sermon and I'll run the exorcism. Sorta like double coverage, don't you think?"

The Rev. Potter considered the idea while the two of them enjoyed a glass of sacramental wine, and then suggested, "Wouldn't it be better to call it an Ecumenical service? That way neither of us will take the rap for bridging the gap—I like that; take the rap for bridging the gap—real alliterative, don't you think?"

"Sounds like a good plan to me, Clarence," said Father O'Toole, as he swallowed his second glass of wine. "When shall we schedule it? There's a full moon right now, and I always get my best mileage when I run an exorcism on the full of the moon."

Thus it came to pass that one of the very first Ecumenical services was performed outside the wall of Old Town Cemetery, but not without some untoward after-effects. Because the cemetery was a town cemetery, and therefore non-denominational, the Baptist rector questioned why he had not been invited to perform as well, on the off-chance that one of the occupants might have been a Baptist?

"We can't let just everyone in on this thing," observed the Rev. Potter. "If we did, we'd have to invite everybody, and before you know it, the Christian Scientists would insist on participating. There'd be no end to it." Thus was laid the foundation for yet another running controversy in town, but that's another story.

The real problem arose over the latent interest on the part of the Historical Society. This group of worthies learned of the matter somewhat after the fact, and bent on catching up, threatened the town with litigation unless it, the Historical Society, was permitted to conduct what it characterized as research into the antecedents of the residents of the vault.

"And just how do you people propose to do that?" inquired the Sexton of Cemeteries, who claimed jurisdiction over the subjects, even though they were situated somewhat outside the limits of his preserve. "Are you proposing to ask them?"

"Don't be silly. Of course we don't propose to ask them. They're too senile to give a useful response," said the chairman of the

Society. "We propose to conduct a scientific examination of the remains; carbon dating and all that sort of thing."

"Well, O.K., but you'll have to move fast, because I'm directing the road agent to seal the damned thing up," he retorted.

Just how the affair will eventually end is problematical. The chairman of the Historical Society demanded a fragment of the remains upon which to perform carbon dating.

The Sexton gave him a shinbone from a deceased cow that turned up in the topsoil the Road Agent had recently delivered to the cemetery. The results of the carbon dating seemed to indicate that the sample submitted for analysis is inconsistent with the known facts, thereby leaving the whole issue up in the air.

Old Tink Frothingham, age 96, says he recalls his great-great grandfather saying that when they buried the last murderer hung in town back in 1762, there was room for only one more in the witch-hole. He thinks the other two were witches. "Murderers or witches—all the same to me."

For the handful of people who attended the exorcism, the event was described as a beautiful service, in keeping with the lives those poor souls led.

Following the service, the King's Daughters served tea in the parish house.

# State vs Crampton

Jim Crampton lived with his mother, Hester, who lived with her mother, the Widow Rantilla, on the Nashua Road outside town. Jim was the result of the unscheduled union of his mother with some fellow she thought was named Crampton. Jim was the only evidence that any such person actually existed.

Growing up in this household was not a piece of cake for Jim. He had identity problems, which he solved by working out until he became a very powerful 19-year old. His muscular physique gave him an air of authority he sorely needed. He entertained thoughts of entering the Golden Gloves championships, but his mother was not enthusiastic, being herself totally involved trying to earn a living for the three of them. The last thing she needed was to act as a second for a budding pugilist.

Jim dropped out of high school, and being at a loss for anything more productive to do, he hung around town, during which he discovered beer. This was before the time of rampant teen sex— though his mother had not found that a limitation.

Jim came to the attention of the Municipal Court by way of a complaint for assault and battery, lodged against him by the Rev. Casper "Bones" Jones, the ascetic Chief Pilot of the Alternative Church, a newly formed splinter group to which his mother and grandmother belonged. When the matter giving rise to the events herein described came up for hearing before the Municipal Court, the facts unfolded somewhat along the following lines:

On New Year's Eve, Jim went to a party with some of his friends and didn't come home until around 11 a.m. New Year's Day, well-oiled. Both his grandmother and his mother were beside themselves, and called the Rev. Jones for assistance and counsel.

"Bones" Jones eventually arrived on the scene, and did whatever it was he was accustomed to do in such instances, only to discover it was utterly useless. By this time, Jim was determined to return to the company of his friends and went out the door, pursued by the Rev. Jones and his grandmother. His mother started out to enlist the help of the nearest neighbors, but not before Jim, in an effort to stop her, grabbed her by the blouse and ripped it off, along with certain other garments peculiar to women.

By this time everyone was outside, and Jim, in his desire to apprehend his mother, pushed his grandmother aside. She fell against the Rev. Jones, and the two of them wound up jackknifed in a snowbank beside the driveway with the grandmother wedged in on top of Jones, a posture from which neither of them could extricate themselves.

Hester was unsuccessful in her efforts to enlist help from the neighbors. The only one she encountered was a man of 86, who was so put asunder at being propositioned by a woman so obviously displaying her attributes that he called the local police.

New Year's Day is not a day when any official services are at maximum strength or efficiency. Most of them are volunteers, and the only one on call was Ray Givens, a retired telephone company district manager, whose radio call was A-2. On receiving the call for assistance, he detoured to pick up the judge of the local court, who he knew would be up and about. A-2 wanted a backup in case anything real happened. Together they went to the site on the Nashua Road in A-2's WWII jeep.

On their arrival they found Hester running down the road, everything akimbo, shouting "Jim's drunk! Jim's drunk! We need help!"

A-2 immediately put out a radio call for reenforcements, which arrived not long after in the form of State Trooper O'Brien, who just happened to hear the call on his scanner, and being nearby, responded without getting prior authority from headquarters in Concord. There was now ample manpower to handle the situation, or so everyone thought, until they sought to take Jim into protective custody. He would have none of it.

Trooper O'Brien tried to get handcuffs on him but only succeeded in making matters worse by further irritating Jim. It finally took all three of them to get Jim spread-eagled across the hood of A-2's jeep, with O'Brien holding down one arm, and A-2 and the judge holding down the other. A-2 managed to reach his radio and called for Doc Pottle to come and administer a sedative, or they'd all be there until Jim sobered up.

Doc arrived almost immediately. He was really a frustrated fireman and was listening for fire calls on the local radio net when he heard A-2 s call for assistance.

"Just you fellows keep holding him there and I'll give him a tranquilizer," Doc said, and he did. In fact Doc gave Jim two tranquilizers before anything happened at all, and then it was only a modest response—just enough to enable O'Brien to convey Jim to the lock-up in Milford. In a final show of strength, Jim managed to bend the door to the one cell at the lockup so it wouldn't close, but he soon fell asleep, thus rendering the bent door irrelevant.

During all this activity, nobody thought much about, or even realized that the Rev. "Bones" Jones was still buried in a snow bank beneath the Widow Rantilla, who was herself stuck, but more concerned about what the neighbors might think if they got the idea that she had been on top of "Bones" Jones on purpose. If anyone showed up, she'd just have to melt her way out of the problem.

On returning to the scene, Trooper O'Brien discovered the Widow Rantilla and extricated her. To his amazement, he discovered the Rev. Jones, who was by now considerably the worse for wear, since the temperature hovered around ten degrees below zero. It was the Rev. Jones who brought the complaint against Jim.

When the matter came up for a hearing, Jim was all shined up and on his best behavior. In fact he struck the judge as a rather decent kid who had had a difficult time growing up. He had no previous record. His mother appeared ready to do anything to prevent him from getting a record. His grandmother suggested that the Rev. Jones was the one that ought to be on trial. "He's a useless weakling," she said. "Couldn't even climb out of a snow bank."

"With you on top of me, how could I?" retorted the Rev. Jones.

The judge had to take some action but just what it should be escaped him at the outset. He was charged with enforcing the law, but plastering Jim with an assault and battery conviction struck him as a bit stringent in the circumstances.

The issue was finally resolved when it became clear that nobody really knew how old Jim really was. If he had not reached 18, he was a juvenile, and the judge had a lot of latitude. If he was over 18, and therefore an adult, the options were narrower. Hester blushingly admitted that she really didn't know either, enabling the judge to opt for juvenile status. After considerable conversation among the participants, the judge put the matter on file, a disposition he characterized as, "I've read the charge, but so what?"

As this is written, some years after the event, the local newspaper reports that Jim Crampton, formerly of these parts, was recently crowned heavyweight champion of the Sixth Fleet, according to *Anchors Aweigh*, the Sixth Fleet newspaper.

The decisions of the local Municipal Court do occasionally have far-ranging consequences.

# The Town vs Five Beavers

Anyone who thinks that life in today's world has reached the pinnacle of complication really hasn't lived very long. What happens today, though complex, can't hold a candle to the doings of our immediate ancestors. Those worthies cranked up, and perpetuated, some of the most complex and involved affairs in town history, many of which remain in one form or another to plague local officials.

A notorious flap of this sort involving our town, it's immediate neighbor to the north, the state game warden and five beavers promises to go down in legal annals as one of the most durable causes yet devised by the mind of man, or beaver, with little or no prospect of settlement within our lifetime.

The whole thing started when a family of beaver elected to build a beaver housing development upstream of a small bridge on the back road connecting Whiteacre with the town of Blackacre. The actual names of the two towns are disguised to comply with an order of the court not to reveal any of the details of the case, including the parties, in order to avoid unduly inflaming the populace of either of them.

The bridge, the center of the controversy, was typical of many back-road bridges spanning small streams, in that it consisted of a casual assemblage of granite slabs, used because they were readily available locally. Some say granite was used because it enabled the builders to display their native talents as stone masons, a skill developed over the years trying to farm the rocky soil.

The region was at one time the granite center of the entire world, and a goodly supply of randomly shaped slabs remain at the sites of some of the old abandoned quarries. The road agents of the surrounding towns help themselves to this material as an alternative to paying for building materials, thereby extending their budgets, which makes them look good at election time.

Unfortunately, granite doesn't come in sizes. You have to make do with whatever sizes are kicking around. This produced some pretty short bridge spans. Flooding upstream due to the narrow waterway beneath the bridges, together with an ample supply of brush and saplings, created conditions no sensible beaver could possibly ignore—and they didn't. They built a gigantic dam upstream of the granite bridge on the back road that connected the two towns.

With the passage of time, the beaver dam seemed to expand, along with the increasingly affluent population of the town. Like the town's two-legged citizens, the beaver were propagational experts. What began as a pair eventually developed into a tribe. The original beaver dam became a beaver condo.

As is the case in the puckerbrush, spring brings melting snow to flood the brooks and tributaries, including the one the beaver had chosen. For ten months out of the year it did little more than quietly flow beneath the granite bridge on its way to the Souhegan River. During the other two months, it became a raging torrent, overflowing its banks and eventually flooding the road itself, rendering it impassable.

The usual practice in such a situation is to post a sign on the approaches to the bridge saying "Bridge Impassable Due to Flooding," and let it go at that. Being a back road, nobody of any consequence uses it anyway, and those that do just splash right across, hoping their vehicle won't conk out. The Whiteacre Road Agent didn't figure he could do much about it anyway, at least not " 'til the water goes down and then it won't make no difference anyhow."

At a Whiteacre Town Board hearing on the matter, he cited a little-known statute that he said covered the situation, pointing out to the Selectmen that the town line runs right smack through the middle of "that there bridge, so Blackacre is just as responsible as we are, and anyway, they're on the upstream side. Can't do nothin 'til they get rid of the beaver dam on their side."

So nothing whatsoever was done to correct the problem until Old Pop Tuttle, a local farmer and one of the last of his breed still holding out, came storming into a Selectmen's meeting, demanding that the problem be rectified at once.

"That rud runs right by my farm, and I use it ever week when I go ta Manchester the back way. I pay my taxes and I'm damned well goin' to see that you boys maintain the public highways in this here town!"

By the time Pop finished, he was in a lather. The Selectmen's room smelled strongly of manure, and the Selectmen themselves pushed away from their table as Pop leaned across it to emphasize his point.

"I'd shoot the danged beaver myself if it weren't agin the law!" he shouted. "All ya gotta do is call the State Game Warden. He'll blow up the damn dam, and that'll end the problem!" With that, he stormed out of the room in a cloud of grain dust.

Neither the Selectmen nor the Road Agent had seen hide nor hair of the State Game Warden since he wandered into town last spring to deliver a Have-A-Hart woodchuck trap to Henrietta Dingle, local gardener and animal-rights activist. However, it was worth a try, so they wrote a letter to the Fish and Game Commission in Concord, requesting the services of the warden assigned to the county, requesting that he be directed to deal with a certain beaver dam threatening life and property in Whiteacre, namely one bridge on the Col. Wilkins Road.

The First Selectman pointed out that unless you say that life and property are endangered, they'll respond with evolutionary speed, because after six terms as Selectman, he knew whereof he spoke when it came to state agencies.

In accordance with its usual practices, Fish and Game didn't reply for several weeks even in the face of imminent crisis, which in this case was the arrival of Pop Tuttle at Fish and Game headquarters, to determine if the Selectmen really did their duty as he suggested they should.

Pop discovered that they had, but that Fish and Game hadn't quite gotten around to doing anything itself. Fish and Game relied on the well-founded theory that given enough time, nature corrects its own problems, whether Fish and Game intervenes or not. What they hadn't counted on was Pop, who then let them have both barrels when he discovered nothing had been done. So shaken were the Fish and Game people when Pop got through with them, that they assigned their best man to the problem, one Percival "Sonny" Howard, an ardent outdoorsman, conservationist and explosives expert, reputed to be skilled in dealing with beaver dams.

Not much is known of the procedure Sonny used, other than that he tried several times to remove the beaver dam with conservative amounts of dynamite before resorting to what he later described as "my mega-charge." Even then it took him three shots, the last of which not only eliminated the beaver dam, it also took out the Col. Wilkins bridge. All that remained after the smoke cleared was what certainly appeared to the casual observer to be a large crater, filled with water and featuring chunks of granite arranged in a random pattern around its edges.

Sonny made one of his characteristically understated reports back at headquarters, saying "damn dam job done."

Upon hearing the final blast that eliminated the beaver, the dam and the bridge, Pop Tuttle went to investigate, only to find the Blackacre Road Agent already on the scene. Thinking Pop had caused the devastation, the Road Agent berated him for destroying an inter-town bridge, stating, in addition, that the Revised Statutes provided for both civil and criminal penalties for anyone as much as thinking about doing such a thing. He further asserted that Blackacre certainly would bring suit for the replacement of the bridge, since it was an inter-town bridge, and that Blackacre wouldn't share in the cost. "Ain't commin' out of my budget, not by a long shot," he concluded, as he jumped back aboard his road grader and peeled off.

It certainly appeared to Pop that he not only managed to get the beavers displaced but that somewhere along the way he'd be able to enjoy a new bridge. He didn't quite like the suggestion of criminal penalties, but the Whiteacre Selectmen would have to deal with that problem, not Pop. After all, he didn't set off the charge that finally did the job on the bridge.

Whiteacre's Selectmen, none too eager to tempt fate, did what Selectmen habitually do—nothing whatsoever. During the summer, the Road Agent occasionally brought up the subject of the bridge, but as usual, nothing much came of it. Newcomers to town seldom if ever used the road, and unless and until somebody pressed the matter, why spend money to fix it?

However, the issue was raised by Pop Tuttle, when he got sued by Blackacre as a result of that town's road agent's mistaken belief that it was Pop who blew the bridge. Pop showed up at the Whiteacre Town Hall with his lawyer, one Charles J. Oldfamily, Esquire, a member of the staid old firm of MacTavish, McGovern and M'God, the omnipotent firm in Manchester.

Oldfamily, in furtherance of his client's cause, piously advised the Selectmen that he contemplated interpleading the town as a party defendant in the action against his client for the destruction of the inter-town bridge unless they took immediate steps to replace it. He further suggested that their failure to address the matter in their capacities as selectmen might, in his considered opinion, subject them to personal liability for dereliction of their duties.

The Selectmen, being cognizant of the random ploys that lawyers habitually indulge in, especially when they're working on a time-and-charges basis, elected to do nothing some more and await further developments. Until the town itself was actually sued, Town Counsel couldn't start his meter running too. Given the usual propensities of the legal profession, that in itself was a significant saving.

However, Town Counsel, himself suffering from a brief shortage of business, was interested in encouraging the litigation, an undertaking at which he was a past master. Upon receipt of the Bill of Interpleader, formally involving the town of Whiteacre in the suit by Blackacre against Pop Tuttle, he adopted his standard ploy of filing a motion alleging misjoinder of parties, and seeking dismissal of the action against the town, while leaving Pop on the hook. Somewhere he figured the doctrine of Sovereign Immunity could be pulled out of the hat, even if everything else went against him. Furthermore, a motion of this sort calls for a hearing, which most judges tolerate with only a modicum of displeasure, because they were once lawyers too.

Suspecting that maybe he had moved a bit hastily, lawyer Oldfamily decided to see what the case was all about, by reviewing the known facts. He learned that the bridge was actually destroyed as a result of certain miscalculations on the part of one

Percival "Sonny Howard," the State Game Warden, when he calculated the quantity of dynamite to use against the beaver dam. This prompted Oldfamily to join the State Fish and Game Department as party defendant, thereby adding the Attorney General to the list of lawyers appearing in the case.

The Attorney General, being singularly devoid of humor, filed a motion seeking dismissal of the action against Fish and Game on the ground of Sovereign Immunity, though it took him eight pages to do it.

Town Counsel, fearing that this Sovereign Immunity thing might prove troublesome if someone else used it, moved to join Percival "Sonny" Howard as a party defendant, alleging that in using excessive quantities of dynamite, Sonny exceeded his authority as a game warden, thereby subjecting him to personal liability.

Sonny was covered by a homeowner's policy which, among other things, protected him from an assortment of difficulties any normal homeowner might experience, but not the use of excessive amounts of dynamite in the performance of his official duties as State Game Warden. The insurance company filed a Bill in Equity seeking a Declaratory Judgment by way of a finding that it didn't have to defend Sonny because the claim was beyond the scope and coverage of the policy. Sonny hired a personal lawyer to defend him, and he asked for a hearing on the insurance company's motion.

Whiteacre Town Counsel, having by this time lost the thread of the case, filed a motion asking for a pretrial hearing to, as he said, "reduce the various issues to coherent proportions." Counsel for all the other parties opposed this motion. Lawyers never like to have issues clarified, on the off-chance that the triviality of the entire case is revealed.

The Selectmen of Whiteacre, correctly visualizing their Town Counsel well on the way to building a career out of the matter, suggested that perhaps he'd better get a grip on the case, because their budget item covering legal fees and dog damage were both lumped together, and the recent ravages of certain unnamed town dogs had minimized the prospect of Town Counsel getting paid much of anything unless he took a more realistic view of things.

Spurred on to new legal heights, some said as a direct result of the paucity of funds available for paying his fees, Town Counsel arranged for a pretrial hearing, before "some idiot files something else."

In the inordinate time that always passes between the filing of such motions and their hearings, the bridge got rebuilt. The selectmen of both towns, being mindful that they had already run up legal bills in excess of what a new bridge would cost, decided that contributing equally to the project was cheaper than continuing to fiddle with all the lawsuits. They were getting older and none of them wanted to pass out of office with anything like a protracted lawsuit to deal with on their own time.

Town Counsel, in the interests of what he called legal housekeeping, attended the pretrial hearing, suggesting to the judge that "perhaps the court will regard this matter as mute, since the bridge is already rebuilt." In so doing, he managed to rack up another four hours of billable time, three of which were consumed waiting for the hearing to begin.

Such is the nature of things that although the main issue was disposed of, the case promises to endure. Pop Tuttle has filed a suit for slander against the Blackacre Road Agent. Pop claims his reputation has been sullied by the Road Agent's suggestion that Pop blew the bridge in the first place.

"Hell, if'n I'da done it, he'd a never knowed it," Pop asserted, which everyone agreed was true.

# The Great
# Corpse Crisis

Most small towns have a cemetery or two, devoted to memorializing the shortcomings of the medical profession, to say nothing of certain disadvantages associated with old age. Over the years nobody has been able to circumvent both of these conditions forever, thus accounting for the persistent, if gradual, expansion of cemeteries, a trend that is especially noticeable in those towns that experienced the devastation of the flu epidemic after World War I.

To accommodate this pressing need, the local cemetery, Meadow View, undertook an expansion program that—though slowed by the reluctance on the part of the younger, more Yuppie taxpayers, who entertained the notion that they were destined to live forever—nevertheless moved forward. The Yuppie money-manager types who advanced the idea that to spend tax dollars without any prospect of a return on the investment is contra-indicated, were countered by various comments from the floor, among them being, "If'n you don't fix up the buryin' grounds, *I'll* see ya get a return! I'll come back 'n haunt the hell out'n ya!"

Fortunately, the various expenditures were approved after Ezekiel Crampton, the local town indigent, warned, "You cain't just kick us around 'til we git lost. That might be OK durin' winter, but come spring, boy, you gotta plant us somewhere."

The cemetery expansion, undertaken by a committee consisting of the local undertaker, the president of the D.A.R. and the parson of the Congregational Church, did their work exhaustively and well. Among the features the committee approved was a mausoleum-like structure set in a knoll in the cemetery. The thing was craftily designed so that during the dead of winter when the ground was too frozen to dig a proper grave, the appearance of a conventional burial could be conducted by lowering the casket through a trap door in the top.

In the spring, after the ground thawed out, the casket could be removed through a door on the back side, and a conventional burial could be accomplished. The undertakers pointed out that not digging graves in the dead of winter, when the ground was frozen, would eliminate the need to bring in a compressor and a jack hammer for a day, just to get below the frost line. Reminding people of the way frost has a tendency to force rocks to the surface, and "It'll do the same thing with caskets," carried the day.

The winter vault was duly constructed and served its purpose for a number of years, acting as a way station between Here and There. In fact it worked so well that neither Protestant nor Catholic ever raised a question—the Unitarians apparently didn't give a damn one way or the other—about its suitability until quite recently, when all hell broke loose. Before the affair finally subsided, several leading lawyers got involved because, as one of them noted, "This is the sort of case where there is no downside. If you lose, egos are satisfied, and if you win, there's money to be made," a fundamental tenet of the legal profession.

The whole problem began when Ezekiel Crabtree, one of the town's more abrasive characters, finally gave up the unequal struggle against advancing age and passed away at 94, as a direct result of having fallen out of his hay loft. He didn't linger very long, and his next of kin wanted to get the service out of the way in a hurry to avoid unnecessary expense. Furthermore, a nor'easter was blowing up, and the prospect of having to attend a funeral in a blizzard was not appealing. The women, who had cooked up a goodly feast to celebrate the occasion, didn't want it to go to waste if attendance was scanty due to the weather.

"Planter Paul" Snodgrass, the local undertaker, made all the arrangements. "Burial will be in the winter vault," he said, "with final interment in the spring, when the ground thaws out enough to dig him in."

A helpful neighbor suggested, "Why not just leave him out on the ground? Where he's going, he can just melt his way down until the Devil discovers he's dead and comes up after him."

On the appointed day, the temperature hovered around ten below zero. The east wind blew in great gusts and piled the snow in massive drifts. It was not the sort of day anyone would want to linger in the cemetery, but if the parson had his act together and didn't waste time, the whole thing could be accomplished before everyone froze to death.

The procession to the cemetery moved along with all due deliberation. Leading the way was Planter Paul and his assistant, Jeb, in Paul's Pontiac combination, a vehicle used as both a hearse and an ambulance—usually in reverse order—just by switching the flip-flop sign on the side.

In his haste, Paul neglected to make the switch, giving rise to such comments as, "Good grief, you don't suppose old Zeke is still alive, do you?" and, "I didn't realize he was a Christian Scientist," and, "Maybe they didn't embalm him. Maybe they just left him outside and froze him up instead; that might account for it."

Paul had a bit of a problem backing the combination up to the vault's trap door at the top of the hill. He eventually made it, but a bit off to one side and deep in a snow drift. The mourners plowed through the snow on foot. Parson Tuttle immediately began racing through his oration, his wife holding on to his coattails to keep him from slipping through the trap door himself.

Undertaker Snodgrass was a perfectionist. He wanted nothing more than to be known as the man who conducted the best funerals in town. To make doubly sure, he sent his assistant, Jeb, down the back side of the hill to enter the vault by its lower door in order to remove the slings from the casket once it was on the floor, so they could be retrieved from above without causing too much commotion. Under normal circumstances, this would have been a routine procedure, capable of being carried out by any average undertaker's mute without assistance or supervision.

Unfortunately, the nor'easter had reached violent proportions, with the wind blowing at gale force. As the assistant opened the lower door of the vault, a great gust swept in, causing the casket to swing around like the pendulum on an eight-day clock. It knocked the assistant out cold, smashed the casket against the granite wall of the vault, and dumped old Zeke right out on the floor where he lay amid a pile of what was now kindling wood—just the sort of thing Planter Paul hoped to avoid.

But by then, Paul was engaged in trying to extricate the combination from the snowdrift before it got completely bellied down, frozen in, or worse. He didn't notice the absence of his assistant, since the trap door was now closed and presumably everything was in order below. It was only after he had returned to his funeral parlor that he noticed his assistant was missing, and returned to the cemetery to look for him.

By this time the assistant had come to and discovered that he was trapped in the vault. The snow had built up around the door, so he elected to try an escape by climbing out through the trapdoor above. It was during this effort that he came to the attention of Rocky Crampton, who, passing the cemetery on his way home from work as a sawyer at the local lumber mill, noticed the trap door suddenly burst open and a ghastly figure emerge, only to slip on the ice and snow and fall back through the opening just before the trapdoor slammed back down.

"Could it be," thought Rocky, "that Doc Klaxon was a bit hasty in his recent diagnosis?" The momentary picture Rocky had of the figure as it disappeared back down through the trap door certainly looked just like old Zeke when they loaded him in his box.

Rocky called the Chief of Police, saying, "Chief, you'd better get right down to the buryin' grounds, cuz I jes seen ole Zeke trying to climb out'n the vault. If you hurry, maybe you'll be able to stuff him back in again before anyone notices he ain't quite dead yet."

Chief Barton, not wanting to get prematurely involved in what certainly appeared to be a developing situation, nor go out in the blizzard for that matter, delayed long enough to finish his coffee, which as events transpired, gave Paul time enough to reach the cemetery, discover the enormity of his problem, and race back to his shop to pick up another casket. He left his assistant on guard to ward off the possibility that some stranger would wander onto the scene and become privy to an undertaker's worst nightmare.

By the time Paul returned with the replacement casket for Zeke, the assistant was nearly frozen himself. To keep warm, he had started a fire with the remains of Zeke's splintered casket, causing smoke to seep out through the trap door. It was the smoke that first caught the attention of Chief Barton and his second in command as they waded through the hip-deep snow toward the vault.

"I hope you went to church today," said the second in command.

To which the chief replied, "Maybe we'd better go back and get Father O'Toole to run an exorcism before we do anything more. Better be safe than sorry, you know." With that, the two officers of the law returned to the station for reinforcements.

On their way back to the cemetery, the Chief and his reinforcements passed Planter Paul and Jeb, the assistant, in the combination heading back toward town, after installing Zeke in a new box
and firmly locking the vault. The chief and his men subsequently
found nothing amiss at the cemetery, and recorded in the police
log, "False alarm—cemetery."

It took Paul quite a while to warm up his assistant, once they were
back at the undertaker's parlor. Paul called the assistant's wife,
suggesting that maybe she'd better come pick her husband up, in
light of the events of the past few hours, explaining in detail what
had transpired.

"You should've left him right there," she said, "that would have
been the high point of his life."

There remains, however, lingering speculation on what Planter
Paul will find when he returns to complete the interment in the
spring, but that's another whole story.

# The Winter Vault Caper

Until fairly recently, there wasn't much call for a formal, full-time police department in our neck of the woods. The elected constable and his roster of specials provided all the protection the average law-abiding citizen really needed. During the week, when the constable was engaged in earning his living as a plumber, the town was covered by the state police trooper assigned to the fifty square miles of southern New Hampshire. Anyone feeling the need for a policeman had only to call the state police communications center in nearby Milford, and the chances were better than even that the trooper would be somewhere within range of the local radio net. If not, then he could be reached by calling Concord, which would get him on the state-wide network.

As an added source of protection, the local constable had both the local and state police network radios right in his plumbing truck. He'd turn the volume up to high on both radios, and leave the door of his truck open so he could hear the conversations even if he was in somebody's cellar repairing a furnace, thereby achieving double coverage, something he was wont to boast about around election time each year. In short, a call for aid during the week was apt to bring both the local constable and the state trooper.

Until recently, this arrangement worked quite well because the incidence of crime in the puckerbrush was quite low. Places like New York and Los Angeles report more murders before breakfast than New Hampshire generates in a year. Local records seem to indicate that the last one Amherst had occurred back in 1820, and

it didn't require much police work. The culprit was found standing over the victim, holding a bloody pitch fork in his hands,
muttering something to the effect of, "I guess you won't fool
around with my wife again, will you?" To which the victim made
no reply.

Unfortunately, modern criminal activity, which was beginning to
filter down to rural areas, called for a level of investigative expertise and detective work that was beyond the scope of the average
constable's resources. In particular, the arrival of marijuana on
the local scene brought it all to a head. Local tactics had to be
beefed up if this new menace was to be brought under control.

To correct this deficiency, the state police conducted a series of
seminars around the state, which they called Modern Criminal
Trends, at which local constables and their special officers were
schooled and indoctrinated in modern criminal practice and procedure. Such subjects as stakeouts, criminal patterns and profiles,
identification techniques and the elements of white-collar crime
were explained in exquisite detail. Even the Governor showed up
at the final session to award the participants certificates confirm-
ing that they now had the tools to attack the criminals in our
midst.

This was pretty heady stuff for Constable Jenks and his stalwart
specials—Alexander "Rocky" Forsythe, Rufus "Bud" Andrews and
Jonathan "Jock" Tippet. They all came home determined to root
out those criminals the Governor had in mind. Morale was at an
all-time high in the local constabulary.

And it was none too soon, because Jenks and his staff were rudely awakened to the modern criminal's new and sinister trends. The highly specialized marketing practices of the marijuana merchants rendered prevailing police tactics totally inadequate to cope with the escalating menace. The appetites of a whole new breed of overachievers, who came to town to escape the ravages of whatever it was they came from, required more sophisticated tactics. Their kids were worldly beyond their years and brought with them desires they had acquired elsewhere—including a devotion to marijuana. It wasn't long before the odor of pot smoke overpowered the smell of dried manure seeping from beneath many of the restored barns around town.

"It's here," said Constable Jenks, "we just have to find it. Can't miss that stink."

Rocky Forsythe suggested that maybe his hound-dog Maggie could be retrained to sniff out the nasty weed. "Then all we'd have to do is chase Maggie around town until she hit it," he said.

Bud Andrews said that would never work. "Maggie howls like a banshee when she's onto somethin'. You can hear her for half a mile. You'd never manage to catch anyone; she'd alert your quarry long before you'd ever get to them."

For the next week or so, nothing happened. Constable Jenks was said to be overreacting when he sent several samples of grass-like material, taken from the back of Sy Comb's pickup truck, to Concord for analysis, only to learn that it was hay, and not what he had suspected. Nor was the problem viewed as a particularly pressing one until Rocky Forsythe, retaining an owner's confidence in the capability of Maggie, had a hard time dragging her away from the winter vault in the cemetery behind the town hall. She had jumped out of his pickup truck while he was attending the weekly Special Officers Strategy Meeting with Constable Jenks.

"Anybody stored in the winter vault, Chief?" he asked, as he carried Maggie back to the pickup. "Good thing the door was only ajar, or Maggie'd been right inside," he observed.

"That door ajar?" asked Constable Jenks. "That thing is supposed to be closed tight. If there's as much as a crack in it, the coons'll get in and raise hell with whoever is stored there. Nearly devoured poor old Clem Pickle two years ago, you know. Better check it out."

In order to grasp the significance of this seemingly trivial event, it is necessary to know that most New England towns have a winter vault in the town cemetery. This feature, set in the side of whatever hill is available, is used to store the deceased if they happen to expire when the ground is frozen solid, making the digging of a proper grave difficult if not impossible. Until the spring, when the ground thaws out enough to carry out a proper burial, local undertakers store their clients in the winter vault.

Except when someone is placed in the vault or taken out, the iron door is always closed. To discover it ajar this late in the year called for further investigation.

Constable Jenks first consulted Clem Whipple, the Sexton of Cemeteries, to see what he knew about the matter, and he did. Clem was a charter member of the AARP, and as an alternative to Metemucil, he kept regular by mowing the grass in the cemetery.

"Yas, I know'd the door is ajar. I had a couple of kids pry up the latch so I could store my lawn mower in there during the summer. I'm almost 81 you know, and I can't lug the damned thing back to the town barn ever time I use it," he explained. "It's all I can do to start it, let alone cart it back across town when I'm all done."

After inspecting the vault, the Constabulary retrieved the mower and gas can and closed the door firmly. Constable Jenks suggested that the Sexton might want to put a little oil on the hinges, which were suffering from rust, making the operation a two-man

job. He had visions of some undertaker arriving at the vault only
to find he was unable to get the door open.

A week later, Sexton Whipple stopped in to see the Constable.

"Chief, I thought you said nobody was to go inta' the winter
vault, especially after all the ruckus you made about my lawn
mower bein' in there, but when I went to oil them hinges like you
said, the damn thing was open again. Who do you suppose is doin
it? No reason for anyone alive to open it, an' the dead ones
couldn't if they'd a mind to. Jes thought I'd let you know, to give
you somethin ta think 'bout," he concluded.

Clem's revelation certainly did give Constable Jenks something to
think about. At his weekly meeting with his staff, which consisted
of Rocky, Bud and Jock, convened at the Town Hall every Friday
after work, Constable Jenks brought up the matter of the door to
the winter vault being ajar, not once, but twice in one week.

"Boys, they's somethin goin' on in the winter vault, and I think it
may be connected with this pot business. That stuff is gettin into
town somehow, and our winter vault may be the distribution
point. We'll have to set up a stakeout to make sure," he said.

"Golly, Chief, how you gonna do that?" asked Jock Tippet.
"There's no place to hide anywhere nearby without being noticed."

"I've got that all figured out," answered the Constable.
"Somebody's been foolin' around there, and the only way we can
get close enough to see who it is, and nab 'em, is by setting up our

stakeout right inside the vault itself. But we can't just slip in without being noticed. We'll have to get buried just like it was for real, only it won't be of course. Then if anyone sees any activity round the vault, they'll never suspect it's really a plant. Get it?" But nobody did, so the Constable outlined his scheme in detail, after first pledging everyone present to secrecy.

Two days later, Constable Jenks called Planter Paul, the local undertaker, to solicit his cooperation. Briefly put, the plan involved having Special Officer Jock Tippet report to Paul's undertaking parlors, where he would be settled into what Paul called a shipping case, a large metal box used by undertakers to ship caskets, and occasionally their contents, around the country for burial somewhere else. In this instance, the case, with Tippet inside, would be delivered to the winter vault without any formalities, and under circumstances that would attract only minimal attention at best, since no services would be needed for a mere storage exercise. Thus Tippet's presence right inside the vault would go undetected, and effectively booby-trap the scene of the suspected criminal activity.

In order to maintain contact, and incidentally keep him backed up, Tippet was provided with a hand-held radio to call the constable at headquarters, where the balance of the strike force, consisting of Bud Andrews and Rocky Forsythe, would be standing by, ready to sally forth as soon as Tippet reported any activity.

Late the following afternoon, Paul pulled his Pontiac combination up to the winter vault, and with the aid of his undertaker's mute, a wispy little fellow, unloaded the shipping case containing Tippet, and shoved it into the vault. Paul closed the iron door, but was careful not to shove the latch all the way home. Tippet took up his lonely vigil. The stage was set.

The first signs of activity took place around 11:30 that night, when Tippet reported hearing hushed voices approaching the vault from behind the hill.

Constable Jenks called back on the radio and told him to be quiet.

Tippet said he wasn't making a sound, but that the constable, talking on the radio, echoed inside the vault.

The constable told Tippet to turn his volume down a bit.

Unfortunately, Tippet, in trying to reach the volume knob on the radio, spilled his thermos of coffee all over it, short-circuiting the radio, and leaving him completely isolated. He couldn't call out, and he couldn't receive either. Tippet was on his own, though headquarters didn't know this, attributing his silence to following orders. What happened next can best be revealed by Tippet's report to the Constable in the wee hours of the following morning.

"A few minutes after the radio went out, I heard someone open the vault door. I decided that I'd just leap right out of the shipping case, and nab 'em cold. Well, someone did enter, but when I tried to lift the lid on the case, I couldn't even budge it. That idiot undertaker forgot to undo the latches, and I was stuck there, flat on my back. I heard a couple of guys making a buy. Apparently the shipping case didn't bother them a bit, though they didn't linger very long. Assuming they didn't see you coming looking for me, we can use this ploy again, and maybe get lucky."

The following night, the caper was set up again, only this time Tippet fell asleep in the shipping case. He awakened only when he heard the top of the case being lifted as a hand shoved a paper bag inside. Nothing else happened, and the owner of the hand vanished. By 4 a.m. Tippet figured he'd about had it and climbed out.

Examination of the contents of the paper bag the next day revealed a number of packets of straw-like material, which everyone agreed was marijuana. It was a drop shipment in bulk, delivered by a courier, because no local transactions followed.

The problem of how to get the bag back inside the shipping case without attracting attention was solved by the Sexton of Cemeteries. He replaced the bag under the guise of raking leaves around the vault and shoving them inside to get rid of them. Anyone who saw him would think nothing of it, since it was entirely in keeping with the Sexton's usual practices. He was pushing 81, and had a tendency to adopt some unusual approaches to his duties.

Though it was the intention of the constable to have Tippet continue with his shipping-case routine on the ground that he was the only experienced man on the force, Mrs. Tippet flatly refused to permit her husband to spend another night away from home under the circumstances that prevailed.

"If you do that again, I'm coming too," she said. "I'm not going to have you get in that thing alone again; I just won't have it!"

Though Mrs. Tippet was not one of the town's more militant women's libbers, the constable concluded he'd better not put her to the test, even though it meant scrubbing the entire game plan. The transport case was only a one-passenger affair, and couldn't possibly hold two people, dead or alive. Some other approach had to be found if the pot purveyors were to be apprehended.

Again it was the Sexton of Cemeteries who came up with a new idea. He was let in on the scheme to enlist his aid in replacing the paper bag in the shipping case, so security would not be breached if he became further involved. Anyway, as Past Grand Master of the Grange, he could be trusted.

"Why don't you boys just rig up one of those windshield washer things they have down at the garage, only fill it with gentian violet, tie a string to the door latch, and then whoever opens the door will get sprayed purple. All's you'll have to do is hang around until someone colored purple shows up, and then lock him up."

Constable Jenks, revealing his years, observed, "Gentian violet; I remember that stuff from when I was in the Marines in the Pacific. Used it to cure the crud and jungle rot. Damned stuff wouldn't wash off for weeks. Not very high-tech, but it just might work."

He deputized the Sexton as a special officer, and assigned him the task of setting up the ambush, since the Sexton was the only person in town with a plausible excuse for puttering around the winter vault during the day. Anyway, he hadn't oiled the hinges, and this was a good excuse to do so.

Around this time events began to take shape in distant places that would eventually have considerable impact on the entire scheme. Planter Paul, the undertaker, received a shipping case from Florida, ostensibly containing the mortal remains of one Hezekiah Pottle, with instructions to place them in the winter vault in the Meadow View Cemetery, to await final arrangements. This was not an uncommon practice when relatives had to be assembled from distant places.

The Rev. Timothy Jones, along with Paul, both unaware that by this time the winter vault had been booby-trapped by the Sexton, arrived for the purpose of placing the second shipping case inside. As the great iron door swung open, they were both liberally sprayed with gentian violet. However, they completed their appointed task by shoving the second shipping case into the vault beside the first one, and then departed.

The following day being Sunday, Constable Jenks made one of infrequent forays to church, and noticed to his amazement that the Rev. Jones's face and hands were iridescent purple. Could it be, he wondered, that the parson was involved in the pot affair? Certainly would be a good cover, he thought.

"Gosh, Rev'rint, you seem to be under the weather," he commented as the Rev. Jones greeted parishioners at the church vestibule. "Got the crud maybe?"

"No, it's even worse than that. I was assisting the undertaker yesterday in making a temporary interment in the winter vault when we were sprayed with this horrid stuff. I think you'd better keep an eye on the thing. There may be some grave robbers working the area, you know."

Constable Jenks decided he'd better continue the stakeout just to be on the safe side, but how to do it without attracting any more attention was a problem. Fortunately, the Sexton came up with yet another scheme. He proposed digging a new grave in a remote part of the cemetery, ostensibly to receive the new arrival in the vault. If the grave site was far enough away, but in a spot where the winter vault could be observed, relays of the Constable's men could occupy the grave at night and keep the winter vault under constant observation. Radio contact could be maintained with headquarters where reserve forces could storm out at the slightest provocation.

At precisely 1:32 a.m., the Constable, dozing in headquarters, was awakened by Special Officer Bud Andrews, who had the 12 to 4 watch in the grave.

"Chief, I jes' seen a guy go into the vault and he ain't come out yet!" he reported.

A few minutes later he reported again, saying, "Two more guys went in and one come out. They's two of 'em still in there. Wanna nab 'em now?"

"No," Jenks replied over the radio, "not yet. Wait 'til the other two come out and then let me know. We'll nab 'em outside so we don't blow your cover."

The next hour was pretty busy, according to Bud Andrews. "Christ, Chief, this place is like Times Square on New Year's Eve. Better move in now, because there must be four or five of 'em inside this very minute. We can make a big bust if you' ll just get your ass in gear."

Constable Jenks, after consulting his staff, concluded that since his entire crew, including the Sexton, numbered only three, reinforcements were necessary. He put in a call to Milford for their mobile SWAT team, all of whom were at home asleep.

A half hour later, in the still of the night, as distant sirens heralded the approach of reinforcements, Jenks and his men moved out. In the commotion nobody heard Andrews radio from his post in the gravesite. "Tell those Milford guys to shut off their siren; you can hear em all over town!"

By the time Jenks and his staff and the Milford SWAT team had the cemetery surrounded, the objects of their attention were long gone. They too had heard the sirens and beat a hasty retreat. All that remained in the winter vault were two shipping cases, one that recently held Tippet and the one that recently arrived from Florida. The Florida shipping case was chock full of marijuana.

The local newspapers carried extensive accounts of the bust. Constable Jenks and his entire staff were interviewed at length by reporters from as far away as Nashua and Manchester. Estimates of the street value of the haul were on the order to ten grand or more—not much by today's standards, but enough to make local headlines and lend a sense of urgency to certain deliberations of the P.T.A.

Unfortunately the state police have taken over the investigation because it reaches all the way to Florida, somewhat beyond Constable Jenks' jurisdiction. However, flushed with his success, he is now engaged in staking out the old covered bridge over a tributary to the Souhegan River, a structure he regards as the next likely place for crime to strike in town.

Only time will tell.

# Preventive
# Police Work

When last reported, Constable Jenks was engaged in staking out the old covered bridge over a tributary to the Souhegan River, on the theory that now that the winter vault had been blown as a rallying point for the local pot crowd, the bridge was the next logical spot from which they might renew operations.

The Constable had no hard evidence to support that idea, but he told his staff it was just the sort of place he'd pick if he were a pot dealer, especially one who had just been evicted from the winter vault at the Meadow View Cemetery in the center of town. "Anyway, it's easy to scope out," he said, "jes' count who starts across and see how long it takes 'em, and you'll soon get an idea if sumpin's goin on from how long they tarry."

So another stakeout was undertaken from a vantage point in the hayloft of the Widow Martin's nearby barn. Both ends of the bridge could be seen from the hayloft, which contained a couple of tons of hay left over when Bessie Martin sold her late husband's cows. A very comfortable stakeout could be created in all that hay.

The stakeout was a speculative affair at best, requiring that the Constable and his staff create a profile of all traffic crossing the bridge in both directions. Gathering the data from which to distill the profile was a tedious and time-consuming chore, involving shifts of watchers and stakeout reports, together with related police activity, among them being the weekly objective analysis by the Constable and his staff. Nobody really knew what they were looking for, nor did they expect much to develop from the exercise, but it did provide some ongoing activity to justify the overtime the Constable was charging against his budget appropriation.

After about a month of this sort of activity, Constable Jenks had accumulated a vast pile of scrawled notes and reports from his team of watchers. His problem was that he had no idea how to sort the material, or develop any sort of pattern of criminal activity, without which the whole affair was headed nowhere.

"Jeez, Rocky, you've got dozens of reports saying 'Hiram Jones crossed bridge at 4.06 a.m.' What does that tell us?" he asked.

"It tells us that Hiram Jones crossed the bridge at 4.06 a.m. every day I was on duty," Rocky replied.

"So suppose he did; what the hell does that tell us?"

"As I said, it tells us Hiram crossed the bridge at 4:06 a.m. Wha'd ya think I am? a mind reader? That's your job."

It then occurred to Constable Jenks that he might apply some of the sophisticated techniques he learned at the State Police Academy, which ran a course on how to build a criminal profile. Unfortunately he had so much data that he was unable to sort it all out in his mind in any manner that might reveal the criminal pattern he was after. The whole thing was just too complex for him to grasp all at once.

He did think he saw a trend, but by the time he had sifted through all the reports that indicated a trend, he'd forgotten what he was looking for. "The mind of man just can't gobble all this up at once," he sighed. "If we just had a computer, maybe we could make something of it all." But his budget didn't allow for a computer, and nobody on the force knew how to run one anyway.

However, Officer Tweedy, whose wife worked at the local bank, suggested that maybe if the Constable would let her in on what he had and what he was looking for, she could set it up on the bank's computer and run a projection. The computer, she said, had instant recall and could remember everything all at once, enabling it to come up with a trend.

This was viewed as a better approach than enlisting the aid of the town treasurer, whose computer was fully engaged keeping the town's books balanced. Anyway, the treasurer was a notorious gossip, who couldn't keep a secret if her life depended on it. Furthermore, she was writing a book on My Fifty Years as Town Treasurer, which she was confident would be a best seller. These two activities kept the town computer fully occupied.

So it was that the First National Bank became an unwitting participant in the stakeout of the old covered bridge.

Though this activity occurred long before women were recognized as being capable of more than cooking and having kids, Mrs. Tweedy showed unmistakable signs of being bright. She had mastered the bank computer and was periodically recognized for introducing the bank's officers and directors to its capabilities, some of which were disturbing—like the time she analyzed the bank's loan-to-value ratio, and discovered some pretty innovative financing techniques put forward by the local automobile dealer. Her ability to scope out trends with the computer left in question the need for the judgment of the directors at all. She threw herself and the bank computer into the Constable's problem with a vengeance.

After her preliminary run of the data the Constable had accumulated, she reported back that "You aren't giving me anything useful. I need details, details, details. Get me license numbers of all cars crossing the bridge. Get me the times of day when they cross. Get me foot traffic counts. Get me the direction they are going, and when and how often the same car goes over. I need all this sort of stuff to develop a trend," she said. "If there is any sort of recurring pattern of a suspicious nature, I'll pick it up."

About a month went by during which the required data began to accumulate, aided and abetted by successive relays of the Constable's men who manned the hayloft. In fact, the exercise became so highly organized that the hayloft became a much sought-after post for the local force. It was gradually equipped with the comforts of home, including a lawn chair, binoculars and a coffee pot rigged up on an extension cord plugged into the outlet for the abandoned milking machine on the floor below.

It was the coffee pot that led to the untoward termination of the stakeout.

On a change of shifts, some hay was dislodged and fell onto the hotplate that kept the coffee pot hot, setting off what should have been a blaze of sufficient magnitude to consume the entire barn. Fortunately, Officer Ronald Butch Whipple had the presence of mind to kick the whole works right out the loft door, where it flared up brightly in the barnyard below, before being extinguished in wet cow manure.

The barn was saved, but the Widow Martin had had enough. Her attorney wrote to the town and threatened all sorts of horrible litigation, the magnitude of which would have raised hell with the tax rate, just defending it. He concluded with a demand for $6.00 for the estimated two bales of hay consumed by the fire, and $100,000 for what he called emotional damage suffered by the Widow Martin.

Town counsel suggested that maybe the town ought to compromise the claim if at all possible, because "you can't ever tell where something like this can go." The parties eventually agreed to abate the taxes on the barn for that part of the year it was used for the stakeout, lifting a cloud from Constable Jenks's activities.

Naturally, Constable Jenks and his men were somewhat disheartened at this turn of events, but having accumulated such a vast pile of data, they might as well have Mrs. Tweedy run it through the computer and see if anything turned up.

"After all, we've invested a lot of time and effort in this thing, and if there's anything there, we'd like to know what it is," observed the Constable in a belated effort to salvage something from his investigations. "If we can turn up something, maybe some of the surrounding towns can use it. They have the same sort of problem as we have. At least if we give 'em something, they'll owe us one."

Mrs. Tweedy, the urgency of the matter having abated somewhat, began to sort through the Constable's notes and loaded what she regarded as the salient information into her data base. It took her a month or more, because she had to interrupt her work to get out the customer's statements at the bank, in addition to producing all sorts of printouts for the bank officers who had become infatuated with the way she could fine-tune the computer to reveal some pretty startling information about the bank's customers.

"Gorry," one of the older directors observed. "With this thing, we could make the Great Depression look like a boom."

"Or maybe make our present real-estate boom look like what it may become—a complete bust," commented one of the more conservative directors, unaware of the truth of his observation.

In any event, Mrs. Tweedy eventually discovered that a black BMW with Tennessee plates appeared repeatedly in Constable Jenks' notes. Additional facts relating to the BMW revealed that it made numerous trips across the bridge, though at irregular intervals. The irregularity of the intervals struck her as significant. When she remarked about this to her husband, he determined to run a check on all the BMWs in town, where their owners worked and whether they used the bridge to get to work.

This wasn't particularly difficult because at the time there were only three people in town able to afford a BMW, and none of them were registered in Tennessee. In fact none of the owners even went to work; they were all retired and given to wandering around town in Cashmere jackets with silk scarfs around their necks instead of ties. They hardly fit the profile of pot purveyors. "So much for that angle," thought Tweedy, though he did mention it to Constable Jenks.

Jenks decided to circulate one of those FBI-type wanted posters among police departments in surrounding towns on the off-chance that someone would make a connection. He listed the make, model and license number of the suspected vehicle.

As Jenks suspected, one neighboring town was also having trouble with its winter vault. Nobody really knew whether it was being used as a pot transfer station, or merely as a place of assignation for the more durable youth of the town. But the technique there was to discourage this unseemly use of hallowed grounds, not use it as a set-up for a bust.

The technique for discouraging the use of the vault consisted of rigging up a tape player on which the chief played a long series of howls and moaning sounds, on the theory that the younger element might be frightened off if they heard moans and groans coming from someplace where whoever was there was supposed to be dead.

Chief Carswell managed to get about two hours worth of material on the tapes by recording the sounds periodically coming from the drunk tank beneath the police station. A regular visitor to the tank—one Merlin Spike O'Hearn—contributed some of the most convincing dying noises while he was sobering up.

It can be reported that once the forces of law and order had rigged the player in their winter vault, complete with timing device to start it playing around 11 p.m., activity around the cemetery slacked off significantly.

Concurrently, the local Unitarian minister reported a marked increase in attendance at his Youth for Christ meetings, and though he couldn't account for this sudden bonanza, he didn't knock it.

"Do you know, I have people from as far away as Tennessee bringing their children to our meetings this summer, and they are people of substance too. One of the most faithful parents drives a black BMW," he commented. "Must be summer people vacationing, I guess, but as long as I'm getting my message across, I m satisfied."

"Drives a black BMW with Tennessee plates? Must be a new family in town. You didn't happen to notice their plate number, did you?" Chief Carswell asked, as he made a mental note to check this coincidence with the data given him by Constable Jenks. Somehow the mention of a black BMW with Tennessee plates struck a responsive chord in his mind. The pattern revealed by Mrs. Tweedy and the bank computer involved a similar car, he seemed to recall. He resolved to check it out and put a tail on the BMW the very next time in showed up at the Unitarian Church on Youth for Christ night.

The tail brought immediate results. The BMW picked up two youths at the church and drove off in the direction of Wilton, past the site of an old abandoned granite quarry, one of a goodly number of such quarries spread out around town, which in better days was known as The Granite Capital of New Hampshire. As the BMW neared the second, and more remote quarry, it slowed down and two people jumped out and ran toward the quarry. The BMW then continued on its way, eventually getting on the by-pass to Boston, where the tail lost it.

A surreptitious reconnoitering of the old quarry failed to reveal much of anything. About all that was left of the works was an old vertical boiler that used to generate steam to power the derricks and winches, and even that wasn't much more than a pile of rusting iron. Everything else had either burned down or been carried away years ago.

But those kids that jumped out of the BMW had run toward the quarry. Chief Carswell reasoned that he must have missed something. If he could only find out what is was, he'd be in a better position to take some action.

Back at the police station, Merlin Spike O'Hearn was about to be released from the drunk tank for the umpteenth time. Instead of offering the usual warning to Spike, the Chief said, "Spike, you've been around for a long time; know anything about the old quarry?"

"The old quarry? Sure. Used to cool my beer in the deep hole until them damned kids found my line, hauled it up, and drank every last drop. Haven't been able to use the place since. Too much traffic. They even found my stash in the old firebox of the boiler."

Chief Carswell mused about the firebox of the old boiler. "That could be the drop-off point," he thought.

The following day, the Chief, in the guise of a lost hunter, ambled into the quarry property from the backside. He had his official badge concealed beneath his hunting license. He walked past the old boiler and peered into the firebox, which contained nothing but a heap of long-dead coals and what appeared to him to be a new plastic bag.

"Now how in hell did a new plastic bag get in there?" he wondered. And then it struck him. The fire box of the old boiler was the drop for whatever illicit trade was being conducted on the property.

Being a full-time, professional police officer, the Chief had been schooled in some of the more modern police techniques, and was well-versed in the legal niceties with which modern criminal law abounds. He could lay on another stakeout, but all he would catch would be the lower level criminals. He was after the big guns. To pick up whoever was driving the BMW, he'd have to have probable cause. Having established that someone had been seen leaving the BMW and running up the quarry road, it was a small step to conclude that the two people who ran from the BMW had put the plastic bag in the firebox. If the bag contained pot, the chain was complete.

That night the Chief and one of his officers, again in the guise of lost hunters, approached the quarry from the woods, retrieved the plastic bag from the firebox, took out a small quantity of a grass-like substance, and replaced the bag. Back in the station house, the substance was confirmed as marijuana by two high school students.

Subsequent events are best revealed by quoting from the local newspaper account of what happened:

> Last Friday evening following the weekly meeting of Youth for Christ at the Unitarian Church, a black BMW car was seen leaving the church, having picked up two youths who had attended the meeting. The BMW drove out the Old Quarry Road, and after dropping off the two youths, was apprehended by the local police, who arrested the driver on a variety of charges, among them being possession of a controlled substance with intent to sell, contributing to the delinquency of minors and operating a motor vehicle after its registration had expired.
>
> The hearing on probable cause was held last Monday morning before Judge Lincoln of the local court. The testimony by the local police was punctuated by

the usual penetrating re-
marks from the Bench:

Officer Whipple: At approximately 9:56 a.m ...

The Judge: Now just a
minute. You fellows always
seem to have the time down
to the gnat's eyebrow, but
then you qualify it by saying
approximately. If you have
it right down to the minute,
why say "approximately"?

Officer Whipple: Nothing is
absolute in this changing
and imperfect world, Judge,
especially when you're involved.

The Judge: Listening to you,
that's obvious. Oh, just get
on with it, so I can lock this
guy up. If I find probable
cause, that is.

Probable cause was found and the defendant was bound over to
the Superior Court for trial.

The case eventually attained considerable notoriety due to the
detailed explanation of the investigative work by the local police.
Though newspapers from Boston carried accounts of the affair,
no mention was made of the contribution the bank made via its
computer, nor the efforts of Mrs. Tweedy, because, as she said,
"The bank wants to maintain a low profile and so do I, in case I
have to do another one of these things my husband gets mixed up
with."

The only one who would have relished some recognition was Constable Jenks, whose initial efforts in connection with the winter vault caper in the cemetery in his town made it all possible, but he wasn't even mentioned.

"That's the last time I share any of my intelligence with those publicity hounds," he said, as he went off to check his latest stakeout behind the pump house at the town well.

# Low Life
# in the High Court

Life in a small country town is generally viewed as bucolic, free from all the miseries generally associated with the urban scene. Out here in the puckerbrush, doors are not locked, keys are routinely left in cars, lost wallets are returned with their contents intact and a general air of civilization prevails. It is therefore unthinkable that in the midst of this pristine existence upsetting events could take place, until something upsetting actually happens. Then the effect can be devastating, ranging from disbelief to outright denial, until it gradually dawns on everyone that a problem actually exists and something has to be done about it.

Coming to grips with anything in a country town invariably involves the entire machinery of government, the churches, the PTA and the Grange. If the problem is severe enough, the Selectmen and even the Municipal Court dip their oars in the water. Once mobilized, these elements constitute a formidable force for good intentions, though it is an even greater problem to demobilize them once the crisis has passed. The awakened players are forever vigilant against the day—not far off in their view, having in mind the escalating degeneration of society—when they will be required again to rise to the occasion.

The matter of the Culvert Kids came to my attention as Justice of the local Municipal Court, which has jurisdiction over juvenile matters, by way of a call from the Road Agent. Things of this nature have a way of materializing from unexpected sources.

"Judge, you'd better get right over here to the Town Hall. I've just pulled a couple of kids out of a culvert under Route 122, just outside town," he said. "They must be from Manchester, because they don't seem to understand English."

On arriving at the Town Hall, I was confronted by two bedraggled waifs, wet, hungry, scared and obviously the worse for wear, sitting on the town road grader, sharing the Road Agent's lunch. They looked to be about the same age as my kids.

"Have no idea who they are, how long they've been living in that culvert, or who they are, but they're sure hungry," the Road Agent said. The way they were plowing through his ham sandwiches certainly attested to the truth of that observation.

"Found 'em because the culvert was blocked up, and I figured we had another beaver problem. The rain last night musta flushed em out," he concluded. We then all trouped into the Selectmen's room at the Town Hall.

"We'd better call the Overseer of the Poor and the Constable to get a handle on this affair. In the meantime, we've got to find somebody to clean them up and take care of them," I said, with unaccustomed authority, as the two waifs stared blankly at me across the table in the Selectmen's room.

"On second thought, that's a pretty cold and callous way of handling this matter. Who else is there in the chain of command around here anyway? These kids need more than administrative attention. Got any ideas?" I asked.

"I'd thought of the PTA, but they've got more kids than they can handle already. How about the Grange? Most of their kids are long-gone, and maybe somebody there might like a little more practice. They all have grandkids, so they should still be in shape," the Road Agent suggested. He then walked out, climbed aboard his road grader and left me, with the two kids eying me warily.

In an effort to establish some sort of rapport, I asked, "And where do you children live?" beginning the sentence with the traditional lawyer's "and."

"Pour vous?" replied the biggest waif.

"For me? No, for you. Where do you live?" I asked again, only to be greeted by blank stares.

Not much progress was made until Yvette Bissonette Callahan arrived, she having been called by the Road Agent. Yvette was the elderly, motherly Outreach Officer of the local Grange. She spoke French, which she learned in her youth in Quebec, before coming to New Hampshire with her parents during the great influx of Canadians to work in the cotton mills in Manchester years ago.

"Don't get much chance to practice my French around the house, you know," she said, adding, "my husband is Irish." That struck me as rather incongruous, but any port in a storm. "Vive le great melting pot," I mused to myself as Yvette engaged the children in an animated, though largely inconclusive, conversation.

"From what I can gather," she said, "they used to live on the back road to Merrimack, probably in one of those shacks in the woods. They say their mother is sick. Better send the Constable out there to see what he can find out," she suggested. "In the meantime, I'll look after the children."

"Good," I thought, "at least the immediate problems sitting in front of me are under control." Yvette took them in tow, saying, "I'll clean them up, feed them and find some clothes for them somewhere along the way. I think the Grange has a box of old clothes left over from our hurricane drive."

That evening a small group convened in the Selectmen's room of the Town Hall to plan the next step. Attending were the Overseer of the Poor, the Selectmen, the Constable, the Judge and a few other people, including the minister of the Congregational Church. Sitting right up front was a woman from the County Welfare Office, on the off-chance that an attempt might be made to foist the cost of whatever had to be done onto the county, rather than on the town. The Selectmen were a crafty lot.

Constable Jenks reported that he had visited the shack on the Merrimack Road and found it vacant.

"I conducted my usual investigation and learned that that the family that had lived there left a month or so ago. Apparently a man, a woman and two children lived there, but they disappeared. Nobody knows where they went," he concluded, thereby adding to the lack of information already building up.

The lady from the County Welfare Office wanted to bring a juvenile complaint right away: "Just to have the necessary paper work out of the way until I can find an adult to serve it on." As Judge, I refused to countenance that action.

"You're not proposing to name these kids as miscreants, are you?" I asked.

"I have to name someone, don't I? Who else is there?" she retorted.

"Well, as long as I'm the judge, we're not going to tar and feather these waifs just so you can develop a file. You county people are always right up front when it comes to bringing complaints, but until someone responsible for this problem emerges, I won't entertain such a thing. Furthermore, Mrs. Callahan is taking care of the kids, and that's what's important to me until something better comes along."

"Is this Callahan person on our approved list? If she's not, she's not authorized to act as a foster mother," said the County Welfare witch.

"I have no idea whether Mrs. Callahan is on your approved list, and I couldn't care less. She speaks French and she volunteered," I observed, "and that's good enough for me."

"I'll have to make an immediate inspection," said Madam County Woman, as she flounced toward the door. "Where does this Callahan person live?"

The Constable pointed southerly, and said, "Out on the Hollis Road."

I thought the Callahan Farm was on the north side of town on the back road to Bedford, but no matter. By the time the County dame found it, we'd have the thing figured out. Or so I thought, but I was wrong.

Further investigations by the Overseer of the Poor revealed that the children were the offspring of a World War II veteran, who overwhelmed a French peasant girl during the Allied push out of Normandy. After the war, he brought the mother and the children to the U.S. with the idea of marrying the mother and settling down to life as a woodsman.

Unfortunately, the marriage never came to pass. The French peasant mother, being lost in a foreign land, took to drink. She never learned English, nor did the father of her children learn French, further complicating the matter.

The father, seeking to escape, re-enlisted in the Army, leaving the mother and the children to fend for themselves in a shack on the Merrimack Road. Unable to converse in English, the mother fell further into the abyss of alcohol, leaving the children to get along as best they could.

How they wound up living in the culvert under Route 122 remains a mystery, but perfectly understandable under the circumstances. The problem was one of finding the mother and trying to rehabilitate her—or so I reasoned.

Mrs. Callahan volunteered to keep the kids for a week or two, until "you find their mother. I have my grandchildren for a week while their mother pops another one, so they'll have someone to play with." That took the heat off the situation for a while, and gave the Constable and the Overseer of the Poor time to track down the mother. I figured she couldn't escape notice for very long, or get very far.

Tales of this sort usually have a happy ending and this one does too, but not before the affair took a turn that forever branded the local parson as a child abuser.

The first cloud that appeared on the judicial horizon came in the form of a Petition to Intervene, filed by the Parson of the Congregational Church. It seemed that before he got religion, he was a lawyer of some sort, and in the highest traditions of that malignant trade, entertained the notion that he and he alone had all the answers.

This, coupled with being a born-again religious fanatic, led him to the conclusion that the over-arching incompetence of the Court to deal with either the practical or spiritual needs of the Culvert Kids required his intervention. Though his petition wasn't couched in quite those terms, he made it plain when I invited him to suggest what entitled him to intervene in the first place.

"I believe that I can bring to bear my highest skills, those of an advocate and those of spiritual leadership, at a time and place where they are sorely needed," he intoned, suggesting thereby that the Court was singularly deficient in both categories.

I've never been one to bother very much about ego—mine or anyone else's—especially when clothed in my robes of judicial office, beyond the reach of the madding crowd below. From this lofty pinnacle, the sharpest jabs by some of the legal trade's most obnoxious practitioners were deflected like water off a duck's back. Muttered remarks such as, "Though I am mindful of the

Court's infinite and totally inscrutable wisdom and logic," were routinely countered with, "I'm glad you acknowledge that this court operates on a higher plane, one which you are so ill-equipped to understand," tended to perpetuate what one local reporter had a habit of calling "one more example of the impenetrable wisdom of the town's judicial wiseacre."

But this lawyer-cum-cleric, operating as he was, neatly positioned astride two fundamentally incompatible trades, called for sterner treatment.

"And apart from your self-admitted skills in these areas, precisely what do you intend to contribute to these proceedings, let alone to the well-being of the two children," I inquired, "assuming I permit you to intervene at all? Are you or your group prepared to assume direct responsibility for these children, including their care and support, until this matter gets sorted out? Or do you just want to be a burr under my saddle?" I inquired.

"I intend to offer my advice and counsel in order that these poor souls not be impaled on the shafts of administrative bureaucracy," he responded, somewhat petulantly.

"Wonderful. Does that mean you plan to second-guess whatever it is this court eventually does? Perhaps you'd like to begin by undertaking something constructive, like finding their mother," I suggested.

"Oh, I have no intention of invading the province of those charged with that responsibility. I propose to function on a more spiritual level," he replied.

"Then perhaps you'd better run back and pray that I know what I am doing," I said. "At least that way the outfield will be covered. I'll appoint you interim guardian *ad litem*. You can take it from there," I said, hoping this would give the Parson enough of a sense of participation to keep him away from doing any real damage.

The Clerk of Court, being a retired Air Force Colonel, dutifully distributed copies of this ruling to all parties, including the shrinking violet from the County Welfare Office.

The County Welfare lady, upon receiving a copy of the order appointing the Parson interim guardian *ad litem*, saw a target and immediately served a complaint and warrant on him, alleging child neglect, along with a host of other indignities, that together provoked a violent reaction. The Parson demanded an immediate hearing on the complaint.

Fortunately the County Attorney, whose concerns were at the time directed at prosecuting the owner of a night spot for selling beer to a minor, requested a continuance, which had the effect of deep-sixing the complaint, from where it has yet to emerge.

In the meantime, the Constable, in pursuit of his official duties, discovered that the mother of the children was lodged at the County Farm, having been picked up drunk while soliciting in nearby Manchester, a double-barrelled offense.

When she dried out and was released, the Constable took her to Yvette's home, thereby solving several problems in one fell swoop. She got along well with Yvette, since they both spoke French. She assumed charge of her own kids, who were by that time starting to pick up English from Yvette's grandchildren.

Her presence in the Callahan household was a great help to Yvette in caring for her Irish husband after his recent stroke—brought on, some say, by his practice of filtering Jack Daniels through peat to give it an earthy flavor, before consuming it in large quantities. In fact she settled in very nicely in a situation that would otherwise have proven difficult for everyone. The whole turned out to be greater than the sum of its parts.

The entire matter eventually dribbled off to an inconclusive conclusion, where it stands today. During all this pulling and hauling, which covered several months, the Great and General Court, as New Hampshire is wont to call its legislature, was in session. With the infinite wisdom this august body often displays, it decided to dispense with Municipal Courts in favor of a system of District Courts. Though this was a long overdue reform, it had untoward consequences.

The County Welfare lady, being somewhat compartmentalized in her thinking, remembered only that her complaint against the Parson had been continued to a later date to accommodate other more pressing business of the County Attorney. She wanted her complaint against the Parson brought forward for a hearing, something the Court refused to do, citing the circumstances then prevailing, but really because the Court was about to expire. She immediately appealed that ruling to the Superior Court.

By the time the Superior Court took up the matter, the local Court had passed into limbo. There was nothing from which an appeal could be taken, decided the Superior Court. She appealed that ruling too, and it received a similar response.

To the best of my knowledge, the entire matter is levitating between a court no longer empowered to do anything, and one disinclined to accept an appeal from a court that no longer exists. The entire matter promises to float in legal space for eternity.

At last report, the Culvert Kids were doing fine. They and their mother have become an integral part of the Callahan household.

Only the Parson remains under a cloud—the unresolved complaint alleging child abuse, something he feels adversely affects his youth activities, given the current publicity about such things in the day-care industry.

However, that's his problem. Justice has otherwise triumphed, though some say by default.

# Friendly
# Cooperation

In most small towns such as ours there exist, in complete harmony with the more established ones, a few groups that can only be regarded as islands of eccentricity. The Ham Radio League and the Inundation Engine Company are typical examples of these unconventional associations.

The Inundation Engine Company is also associated with the Elevation Ladder Company in nearby Hollis. The Ham Radio League is an island unto itself. All of them try to be low-key, but every so often they come to public attention in rather bizarre fashion—totally in keeping with their hidden aspirations.

The Ham Radio League, for example, is presently locked in mortal combat with the Zoning Board of Adjustment over the denial of an exception from the local building code, which limits the height of structures in town to two stories. One of the ham radio boys, who happens to live on the very top of Mack Hill, wants to erect a 100-foot tower on top of his barn, so that his antenna can reach out to the entire world.

The Zoning Board of Adjustment has so far been able to avoid granting the necessary exception to the code on the theory that the Ham Radio League reaches far enough as it is. Additional range would only bring it in contact with the contaminating influences of the Communist world. The League is building the tower anyway, saying it is not a structure within the meaning of the Zoning Ordinance, a move that can only lead to protracted litigation—which the League thinks will serve its purposes just as well as if the Board granted the permit.

The Inundation Engine Company, however, is an entirely different matter. This group consists of a collection of Sparkies who are also dedicated antique car buffs, and who have managed to attain the best of both worlds by combining the two interests. They own an antique Ahrens-Fox pumper, built in 1927 and one that last saw official duty with the Manchester Fire Department before being retired in 1959.

The Fox, as it is called, is a truly impressive machine, in the best traditions of fire truck magnificence. It features a massive, positive-action, four-cylinder piston pump mounted in front of the engine. On top, above the pistons, is a large chrome-plated globe, which acts as the pressure chamber. The whole thing gives the impression of a mechanized rhinoceros in search of prey. In addition, the members of the group have equipped it with all manner of antique firefighting equipment, cadged from cast-off stocks of municipal fire departments from as far away as Boston.

The Fox regularly performs in the Memorial Day Parade around town, to the enjoyment of the scads of kids the group allows to ride on the truck, on top of the hose. It was also a featured ride at the annual Community Fair, though this function was de-emphasized after some insurance creep raised the issue of the liability of the Community Fair sponsors, unless they took out horrendously costly insurance with him.

Though the official town firemen are themselves a spirited group, given to getting their backs up at the slightest suggestion that they are really a bunch of grown up boys playing with big toys, they nevertheless tolerate the Inundation Engine Company and its disparate members. This novel relationship, not shared by any other group in the town, is said to be due to the fact that the Inundation Engine Company contributes regularly to the firemen's relief fund, supports local drives to buy new equipment, and has among its membership some pretty weighty characters such as the local judge and the town dentist. Its Section Leader, Suction Hose, was a Judge of the International Court of Justice in the Hague. Support from such quarters accounts for the two groups working as one in the event about to be revealed.

On the day in question the Fox, as was its custom on Saturday mornings, was engaged in a pumping drill beside a pond at the foot of Walnut Hill. Its hood was raised and the massive four-cylinder engine was pounding away, driving the big pump. Judge Baxter, on one of his frequent visits home from the Hague, and in his capacity as Section Leader, Suction Hose, had 150 pounds of pressure worked up on the gauges. Doc Blivvens, Chief Nozzleman, and his team strained to control the stream of water flowing from the Boston playpipe, a version of a nozzle long ago abandoned by the more modern departments. This activity, and the great arching stream of water, attracted the attention of an appreciative audience of passing motorists who had stopped to watch the show. Cries of "Hold'er, Newt, she be a rarin'," were heard every time Doc swung the Boston playpipe toward the crowd.

Then it happened. The hot exhaust from an orchard sprayer touched off a barn on Walnut Hill, just outside town, and not far from the pond where all this activity was going on. The local fire department responded, stretched out about a mile of hose from the fire to the pond, and put its newest truck, a Ford with a 500-gallon-per-minute pump, alongside the Fox to supply water to the fire. The Ford managed to work up about 160 pounds on its gauges, but couldn't get much more before its engine began to boil. The friction loss going up the hill, and the head pressure in the hose, were too much for it to overcome. A call for mutual aid was radioed to the next town. If the local boys could just hold on until Milford showed up with their new 1,000-gallon pumper, maybe the barn and house could be saved.

But there was the Fox, with its suction already in the pond, putting out a very respectable stream. Could it be that the Fox could get water to the tanker at the blaze?

"Might as well give it a shot," the local chief said. "Just might enable us to hold on till Milford gets here."

Lines were shifted, and the Judge of the International Court of Justice in the Hague managed to work the Fox up to 230 pounds, which was just enough to get water to the tanker serving the fire at the crest of Walnut Hill. Doc Blivvens, having assumed additional duty as Leading Hoseman, patrolled the line from the Fox to the fire and performed magnificently with the help of motorists in replacing a couple of sections of old hose that burst half way up Walnut Hill.

As matters turned out, by the time Milford arrived at the scene, the Fox had been pumping for almost an hour without missing a beat. During that time the barn was lost, but the house was saved. A number of onlookers were soaked to the skin.

As a result of this event, the Fox is now carried on the local fire department equipment list as Pumper Emeritus, in order that it be covered by insurance in case it is called into service again.

To quote the oldest living member of the local department, and old gent in his 90s, "Wish we'd a had'er when the old town hall went up back in twenty-nine."

Framed on the wall of the local fire house is a letter from Judge Baxter, on the official stationery of the International Court of Justice in the Hague, offering his thanks to the local department for affording him an opportunity to do at the grassroots level what he and his colleagues had been unable to do on the world scene—namely, put out fires.

The Inundation Engine Company now basks in a new and totally unaccustomed glory. Such are the ways of rural affairs, and as as one bystander remarked, "They sure don't make 'em today like they use ta."

# A Pervasive
# Privy Problem

*It's impossible to make everything foolproof because fools are so ingenious.* —Periwinkle's Postulate

Every four years, right around national election time, things really begin to heat up in town. In fact they heat up several months before the election, but in the week or so immediately preceding that event, the pace increases dramatically.

Amherst, for some unexplainable reason, is regarded as a bellwether community. Reporters, news anchormen, TV crews and their supporting staffs just plain inundate the place in their relentless pursuit of material illustrating the bucolic, down-home, ruggedly individualistic nature of the natives.

Among them are the wiremen, who hook up banks of phones in the town hall for the print media types. Every news anchor needs a couple of people to lug the camera, carry batteries and line up the citizenry for interviews. Almost every such team has an advance man who makes like he's in charge, smiles all the time and introduces selected locals to the rest of the world. It's easy to get on the front page or the six o'clock news.

Most of these advance people occupy their time between arrival in town and election night by memorializing on tape everything from the church steeple and the cemetery behind the town hall to

192

interviewing the oldest resident still above ground to solicit his views on the candidates.

"And how do you like the candidates this year, Mr. Pottle?" they ask whatever old duffer has been hanging around for just this sort of opportunity to achieve immortality.

"Can't compare to Roosevelt, Sonny. Now there was a candidate! Why, I remember when..."

"Oh, so you're a Democrat, are you, Mr. Pottle?"

"Hell no. I meant Teddy Roosevelt, not that other blivvet!" is a characteristic response to a stupid question, because there are no Democrats in town, and Teddy Roosevelt is regarded as having been a Republican even by today's standards.

"How do you like being the oldest voter in town?" they occasionally ask, to which the invariable response is, "Damn sight better than the alternative."

"And to what do you attribute your healthy old age?"

"Sheer persistence," Pottle invariably replies.

But the real problem arises from the vast number of these interlopers and their retinue of supporting staff. They just can't contain everything they consume while in town, and sooner or later they have to dispose of it. Everybody has to heed the call of nature sometime, and for a town whose sole public facility consists of a two-holer attached to the rear of the town hall, this can present a problem, which it did the year Richard Nixon went in—to office, that is.

Unfortunately, the town hall was built during a more leisurely time, when the town was small, and people having business there did their thing before they left home. Even today there is no sewer system in town, and every house has its own septic tank.

As the town grew, and more and more houses were built, the proximity of the septic systems to the wells providing drinking water eventually led to the installation of a town water system, as an alternative to perpetual green-apple two-step, the traditional ailment of newcomers and visitors who imprudently drank the well water.

The old saw, "It's a great place to visit, but don't drink the water" originated in Amherst. Though this mainly tropical affliction no longer prevails, the sheer number of people arriving in town around election time continues to tax the disposal end of the process.

The town hall retains the old two-holer, mainly because the building abuts the old cemetery, and the attempt a few years ago to upgrade it with a proper septic tank arrangement came a cropper when the plumbers uncovered an unrecorded grave at the very site where they proposed to bury the septic tank.

"Jeez, Henry, there's bones down here. You don't suppose some guy was slid in without paying, do you?"

"Could be, Tom, though the plats don't show anyone planted this close to town hall," replied Henry, the lead plumber. "Jes' keep diggin', 'cause it might be a cow or a horse or somethin'."

"It ain't no horse, Henry, less'n this here horse wore high-button shoes," Tom replied.

Needless to say, this revelation resulted in the abandonment of any further efforts to upgrade the privy in the town hall. About all that could be accomplished was a minor refurbishing of the decor of the interior appointments, and even that encountered difficulties.

The seat was made of a single, wide pine plank, the likes of which no longer exist. Its holes were worn smooth over the years by the friction of countless bottoms. The surfaces had taken on the golden patina characteristic of old pine, especially old pine that had been devoted to privy seats. It was an historical artifact in the minds and eyes of the local Historical Society, which guarded its integrity with a vengeance.

Unfortunately, the years of hard use had taken their toll. The plank had cracked in a couple of places, and it was casually repaired by nailing reinforcing boards on the under side. If used with due consideration for its age and condition, it could be counted on to function as intended for years to come. A lack of reverence, coupled with the pressing need of a portly media type for which it was the sole source of relief, led to a chain of events which are the subject of this treatise.

The whole thing started when the portly TV fellow felt the call of nature at a particularly inopportune moment, and in his haste, he plonked himself down over the right-hand hole. He put his TV camera down beside him across the unoccupied left-hand hole. The combined weight of the two, together with what must have been vigorous efforts of some sort, caused the casual repairs to the antique pine seat to give way with a loud crack, jack-knifing the TV fellow into a small package. He found himself firmly wedged, half in, half out, held fast by the sharp edges of the broken seat, whose points made extrication painful, if not impossible. Being a city type, he began to yell for help.

The first to answer his call was Cy Tuttle, the Sexton of Cemeteries, who, at age 82, lacked sufficient strength to be of much help. He called Red Corcoran, the Road Agent, but between them they couldn't get the TV fellow dislodged. The danger of eliminating any prospect of future generations of TV cameramen was just too great.

During all this time, a cool breeze blew upward from the earthy chamber below, adding to the discomfort of the victim, suggesting to him that unless this situation was cured in a hurry, he stood a good chance of being neutered anyway.

"Please, guys, think of something—think of my wife!" he cried.

Suffice it to say that the victim was eventually rescued, but only after the entire privy was dismantled, and the victim removed by dropping him right through, rather than risk any further damage from the broken boards if any effort was made to pull him back up.

When they finally got him out, he was a sorry sight, no matter how you regarded him. Doc Tinker gave him a tetanus shot; the Grange supplied him with reconstituted clothes and everyone seemed reasonably satisfied, including Civil Defense, which broke into its stores to provide shovels and hip boots. Only the Historical Society bemoaned the destruction of one of the few remaining town artifacts, though everyone else thought the net result was a step in the right direction.

Two months later, and in spite of the fact that Nixon won the election, a stranger arrived in town and went immediately to see the Selectmen, who were meeting to assess the damages caused by the recent election process.

"Are you guys the Selectmen of this town, a municipal corporation?" he asked.

"We're the Selectmen, but what's this municipal corporation thing?" inquired Clem Witherspoon, the new man on the Board.

"Search me," the stranger said. "I'm just the process server, an I got some writs for you boys to enjoy," whereupon he handed an official-looking bundle of papers to each Selectman in turn.

"Golly, look at this thing," Witherspoon said. "It claims we owe some guy called Maury Glutz ten million bucks just because he fell through the privy in this here very building. Wasn't he that fat slob who got his rear end stuck in the privy a couple of months ago? And now he wants megabucks from us? That's gratitude for you. Doc Tinker gave him a free tetanus shot, and now he wants more. Says he suffered vast, permanent injury, humiliation, professional degradation and a lot of other stuff I won't bother to read. This guy fell in the shit and now he thinks he's entitled to come up with the proverbial gold watch."

The matter was handed over to Town Counsel to deal with, he being directed to stifle the thing any way he could—but "don't notify the insurance or our premiums will go up."

Town Counsel, being mindful of his own exposure to malpractice if he dealt with the matter in his accustomed manner, notified the insurance company anyway, but suggested that before they cranked up their machinery, he, Town Counsel, had a plan that might just save the day. After conferring at length with their own, skeptical counsel, the insurance company agreed to go along, but said, "You must keep us advised every step of the way. These New York lawyers are a pretty crafty lot, you know."

The plan involved what can only be called an aggressive defense by way of a counterclaim, alleging all sorts of contributory negligence on the part of the privy-plunger, such as improvident and negligent eating habits that caused him to gain inordinate and unhealthy amounts of weight, failure to act as a reasonably prudent man would have acted under the same or similar circumstances, along with the breach of the civil rights of others entitled to the use of the public facilities.

He was also accused of negligently failing to recognize that the privy was never designed to support something the size of a horse, nor a TV camera to boot. To top it all off, he was charged with the willful, wanton destruction of a significant Historical Artifact, having a value of ten million dollars, for which the town itself sought compensatory damages. A motion for dismissal was also entered on the ground of Sovereign Immunity, though this doctrine was a mere afterthought to gum up the works and give the judge something to think about.

The real thrust of the town's defense was provided by the cross-complaint brought by the town against the TV guy's employer, a national TV network. A notice to take depositions of the network president was prepared, requiring the president, a fellow legally responsible for the negligent acts of his employees but hardly likely to know anything at all about the affair, to appear in the office of Town Counsel in nearby Milford at a time deemed to be the most inconvenient possible for the deponent.

Quite understandably, this tactic to involve a Very Important Personage brought forth a shower of complaints in the form of motions to the court, all aimed at avoiding the need to have the network president interrupt his very busy schedule to appear in some tiny office a long way from New York. These tactics required a protracted series of hearings, attended by platoons of New York lawyers, whose knowledge of local procedure was marginal at best. They may have been hotter than a two-dollar pistol in New York, but up here in New Hampshire, they didn't amount to diddly-squat.

When the matter came up for hearing, they cited decisions from as far away as Alaska and New Mexico in support of their position, but the presiding Judge disposed of them by suggesting, "That may sell in Alaska and New Mexico, but what can you cite right here in New Hampshire?"

When they were unable to come up with anything in the 106 volumes of the New Hampshire Reports, especially on the spur of the moment, the presiding Judge suggested that, "Unless you fellows come up with something I haven't heard of, and do it before 4 p.m. today, I'm going to order your client to give his deposition."

"But your Honor," said the most imperious of the battery of New York lawyers representing the TV tycoon, "our client is a very important and busy man. He has more important things to do than travel up here into the wilderness, just to talk about a broken toilet!"

"As long as his employee, agent and servant can take the time to sue this town of hard-working, conscientious citizens for ten million bucks over what you characterize as merely a broken toilet, then your man can certainly squeeze a few minutes out of his busy day to give his deposition," said the Judge. "Furthermore, the town has filed a countersuit of some magnitude against his network, one that should be enough to grab his personal attention."

On the day of the deposition, Town Counsel was ready. He removed all but four chairs from what he called his conference room, which wasn't any too large to begin with. In fact, his entire office layout paled in comparison to what the New York boys set aside for their janitorial supplies.

The New York contingent arrived in two stretch limos, though only the head of the TV network, the stenographer, and the lead dog of the network lawyer team had chairs. Everyone else had to hang around the limos outside in the parking lot for the next three hours, running up the meter, as they say in New York legal circles.

The deposition did little more than reveal the absurdity of the entire business. Town Counsel eventually filed a motion for summary judgment in favor of the town, along with a copy of the deposition in lieu of the customary affidavit, thereby suggesting that the Court would have little difficulty granting the motion forthwith, once it read the deposition. A taxation of costs was also filed, claiming costs, expenses and reasonable legal fees in an un-specified amount, thereby giving the Judge some latitude to show he had carefully considered the evidence.

Not long after, Town Counsel received a call from one of the minor underlings associated with New York counsel, haughtily suggesting that the entire matter could be resolved without fur-ther complications, if the town would agree to pay the TV ty-coon's legal expenses associated with the network's defense of the Town's claim, which he said amounted, as of this date, to $37,600.

"Our client recognizes the trivial nature of this case, and really doesn't want to expend much money on it," the fellow suggested.

Town Counsel, somewhat taken aback by the size of the quoted fees, especially in view of the fact that he had been able to run up only about $600 himself, nevertheless sensed victory in the wind.

"Well, I suppose we can think about it, but only if your employee will drop his suit against the town and pay the legal fees associ-ated with our defense of that suit, which caused the whole thing."

"I think I can comfortably recommend that to our client. By the way, what are your client's legal fees?" the New York lawyer asked.

"Precisely $465 dollars more than yours," replied Town Counsel.

The Selectmen had some difficulty understanding the nature of the settlement, especially the exchange of receipted legal bills,

and a check payable to the Town for $465, but since the net re-
sult was in their favor, they didn't ask any questions.

The Historical Society undertook the repair of the privy, which
just happened to cost $465, a sum the Selectmen unaccountably
found in their over and short account.

Though this case is not likely to go down in the annals of the law
as a landmark, there are those who seem willing to suggest that it
illustrates the maxim, "The Home Team has the Edge."

# Judicial Reform
# Hits Home

*Come the revolution, things will be different—not better—just different.* —Murphy's Law of Justice

In keeping with its heritage, our town has pounded away with uncommon vigor at the New Deal, the Great Society and the assortment of other social cataclysms that have engulfed the nation from time to time since the the first settlers took it away from the resident natives in the seventeenth century. At the same time, it has treated both the Republican and the occasional Democratic regimes with equal indifference.

Then it happened. The New Hampshire legislature, an aggregation of high-button shoes, more properly referred to as The Great and General Court, undertook to tamper with the system of local justice by abolishing municipal courts and substituting a system of district courts, presided over by full-time judges. The idea was that by consolidating the large number of small, municipal courts into a system of fewer, larger district courts, the ends of justice would be better and more uniformly served. This also added to the patronage pool for the party in power, which was usually Republican. The Democrats have never been notoriously successful north of Boston.

In all fairness, the change was long overdue. With some ninety municipal courts presided over by an assortment of people, both laymen and lawyers, the overall level of legal acumen was spotty.

Some thought this was an advantage, but in the final analysis, they didn't prevail. The following excerpt from the Amherst Town Report for the year the Amherst Municipal Court faded into limbo reflects to some small degree the flavor of an institution that may not otherwise be remembered.

## FINAL REPORT OF THE JUSTICE
## OF THE AMHERST MUNICIPAL COURT

After some fourteen years, during which the great wheels of justice ground relentlessly onward, implemented to some degree by the Amherst Municipal Court, the Governor, in his inscrutable wisdom, aided and abetted by the Great and General Court, has seen fit to render the municipal court system in New Hampshire passé. On July first, the Amherst Municipal Court ceased to exist, its functions having been assumed by the District Court. It is therefore fitting and proper that the Justice, relieved of the necessity of maintaining a judicial demeanor, render his final report in such form as he damn well chooses, with full knowledge that since he can't have his name carved in granite on the Courthouse cornerstone—because there is no more Court—this report will be his Final Hour.

Over the years, there have been the usual assortment of transient breaches of the peace, such as motorists found in charge of motor vehicles while three sheets to the wind, a large number of people who took Route 101 to be a drag strip, those who believed stop signs to be for other people, and those convinced their cars couldn't possibly go as fast as the state trooper said they were going. These cases contained nothing novel or interesting.

However, there have been a few moments of heightened interest—moments that can now be revealed without suffering the penalties of slander, or lack of judicial demeanor, or worse. Therefore, this report will concern itself with those matters, the likes of which may never be repeated, and unless set down for posterity herein, may very well pass into oblivion unheralded.

There was the woman who, for several months, complained loudly about the dangerous and unreasonable speeders on the Mount Vernon Road. These complaints became so bothersome that the state police set up a roadblock just to keep this lady off their backs. The net result of the operation was that the lady who made all the fuss was herself picked up for speeding while going to the post office, and to paint the lily, she was picked up again fifteen minutes later for the same offense on her return trip. She has since moved.

There were several so-called domestic relations matters in which the wife, bloody and shaken, brought charges against her husband because she just couldn't take it any more. Without exception, these cases were dismissed, because on hearing, the sole witness testifying in favor of the husband was the complainant-wife.

A more difficult case was was the one involving complicated issues of conflict of laws. In this case, a chicken house on the Amherst-Milford town line was the scene of a cockerel carnage such as has never been seen since. It seems some animal frightened the chickens on the first floor of the henhouse. They ran from the Amherst end to the Milford end, where they piled up and expired in large numbers. The fracas caused by this event frightened the chickens on the second floor, and they ran to the Amherst end, where they in turn, expired in equally large numbers. The problem arose over which town should pay for the damage. The Town of Amherst took the position that the first floor hens died in Milford, the damage was therefore done in Milford, so Milford should pay.

Milford, on the other hand, claimed all the fuss started in Amherst, and anyway, the second floor flock, though they started their flight in Milford, nevertheless died in Amherst, so Amherst should pay. As far as your Justice knows, the matter is still under advisement.

Nor was the courtroom itself devoid of drama. The court has witnessed the collapse of a chair under the weight of a state trooper, and the suffering of the Judge when he got his tie caught in the zipper of his gown, obliging him to sit through the entire session with his tie hanging out like the tongue on a St. Bernard.

During a conference between the Judge and opposing counsel, conducted in chambers (the kitchen of the Town Hall), counsel for the respondent was so taken with the leftovers from the school lunch program that serious questions were raised about his eating habits.

Aside from the foregoing, and the occasional conflicts with the Ways and Means Committee over who had priority on the court-room—the Court or the Committee—or the time the Grange Whist Night refreshment committee raised a hue and cry over a man the state police had handcuffed to a column in the dining room for safekeeping, things proceeded with reasonable aplomb over the years.

However, vestiges of the Amherst Municipal Court remain. Nobody knows what to do with the pile of old complaints and warrants accumulated over the past fourteen years, and nobody has the courage to throw them out. Perhaps in the distant future some archeologist, digging through the remains of Amherst, will unearth these artifacts and, in learned conference with his colleagues, come to the conclusion that ours was a strange era—nobody ever threw anything away.

Disrespectfully submitted,
C.J. Lincoln, Esq., Justice

# Denouement

In order to suppress once and for all any suggestion that the tales recited in this monumental effort are fictionally inspired, I decided to return to the scenes of my early triumphs and photograph as many of the actual physical remnants as still remained recognizable. Suffice it to say that I discovered that while everything had changed, nothing had changed. It was all still there, only in need of paint.

"You go ahead and do your thing yourself," my wife said, as she headed off for a sale at Jordan Marsh, not far from the Wayfarer Motel, on the outskirts of Manchester, where we were holed up. "Jordan's has a sale going on, and I'm going to see how prices compare with where we live now."

Even at the Wayfarer, things were still the same. Several Moose Lodges from Northern Vermont and New Hampshire were holding what certainly appeared to be a horn-locking jamboree at the place. Great State Beverages was conducting what it billed as The Great Bud Light Distributor Roll-out in the Green Room, and this event spilled over into the Moose affair with predictable consequences. After a while, the Moose hung pretty loose.

My first revelation came as I headed down Route 101 toward Amherst, where so much of my life dribbled away before it tapered off into dedicated indigence. As I passed the Souhegan Sanitary Landfill, concerning which I had something to say in the past, I discovered that it now covers the whole fifty acres of the site originally said to be adequate for the foreseeable future, but is now under some sort of order to close down.

It really didn't need such an order because it was completely full—all fifty acres of it. It resembled the surface of Mars, complete with great hills of soil cover and a dike to divert runoff. It also gave off a certain residual, lilting fragrance all its own.

All this had replaced what had been fifty acres of serene woodland. The local newspaper reported that efforts were now under way to dig the whole thing up and ship it off to Nevada, as the only way to eliminate the hazardous material it was said to contain.

My first stop was at the Town Hall, the scene of so many of my encounters as Judge of the local Municipal Court years ago. What had been the Selectmen's office and courtroom is now the private office of the Town Treasurer. The adjoining kitchen, which doubled in brass as the the Judge's Chambers, no longer exists, having given way to a Mr. Coffee machine, a row of snack vending devices and a microwave oven.

A lady who had been my secretary for a time before becoming secretary to the Board of Selectmen, then Tax Collector, and now the Town Administrator, presides over the whole show from an office carved out of the large meeting room on the second floor. She thought I had died years ago, and greeted me as something resurrected from another world. We didn't have much time to chat because she was dashing off to Concord to see if she could

persuade the Water Supply and Pollution Control Commission
to get its act together and approve the new town sewer proposal.

"We've had a water system for thirty years, as you well know,"
she said, "but now we need a sewer. There's no room for any
more septic tanks in town, and unless we get a proper sewer, the
whole place will just float away. If we'd had this thing approved a
couple of years ago before the fire department consumed the accumulated cash reserves of the water district when it built that
Taj Mahal of a fire house, the entire sewer project would be built
now."

I seemed to recall something about the water district and the fire
laddies some years ago. Apparently nobody votes against the fire
department, even today.

In my effort to get pictures of some of the scenes connected with
my past, I went to the bridge the State Game Warden blew up
twenty-five years ago, and there it was, only modernized for the
second and perhaps the third time. As I was photographing this
monument, a pickup truck with the town seal emblazoned on its
side pulled up, and out stepped Red, the same Road Agent from
twenty-five years ago. Only now he is Superintendent of Public
Works, drives around in a pickup truck, and wears a tie.

"Gee, Judge, I thought you were dead," he said. "Remember the
time the game warden blew hell out of this thing? Had to rebuild
it twice since then. Cost us three hundred grand to do it the last
time; guidelines, you know."

"Gosh, Red, that's a hell of a sum," I said. "Wasn't the bridge you built to replace the one the game warden blew up good enough? There isn't any more water to contend with, is there?" I asked.

"No, and maybe a bit less, but we had to build it to meet the hundred year flood rules, and they're a bitch. Why, I could drive my truck through this waterway today. It's been a great place for the cokeheads to trade wares too. Nobody thought of looking under the bridge for them until recently. Remember the time the constable found the pot crowd using the winter vault in the cemetery? Well, now they operate under this bridge from time to time. Been a big problem, you know," he concluded.

Red also brought me up to date on how the big squabble about the fire horn finally played out. That was the fuss that arose over some pigeons that made a habit of nesting in the fire horn between alarms. Every time they got settled in, they were blasted out when the fire call was sounded, sending them to wherever it is pigeons go when they make the mistake of nesting in fire horns. But this is a thing of the past. The volunteers now have beepers to receive the call to duty. Those out of range of the beepers couldn't get there in time anyway.

The old air-powered fire horn is now an Historical Artifact, displayed along with other fire department memorabilia in the trophy room at the new fire house. Among the trophies on display is the Cyrus Whipple Memorial Coffee Urn. This trophy is in memory of a departed vamp who, it is said, decreed in his will that he be cremated and his ashes placed in a Maxwell House coffee can and displayed beside the coffee urn he tended so faithfully for so many years.

Upon inquiring about the Maxwell House coffee can, I learned that someone had mistaken the contents for the real thing, and brewed old Cyrus up a short time after his decease. Nobody wants to talk about it now.

Still clinging to life is the ongoing fracas over the town clock that provided so many budding orators with an opportunity to spout off at Town Meeting. I picked up a copy of the 1989 Town Report and discovered that, while the issue remains alive, the original flavor of the debate seems to have withered. It has become an administrative matter having to do with some sort of scheme to thwart the traditional New England version of urban renewal called "fire." Somebody wants to have the town contribute to installing a sprinkler system in the church in case the clock catches fire first. The article reads as follows:

ARTICLE 23 (By Petition)

"To see if the Town will vote to raise and appropriate the sum of $5,000 as its share of the fire protection installed/planned by the Congregational Church, or take action relative thereto." (This becomes Amherst's responsibility since the town retained ownership of the clock and steeple when the remaining building was turned over to the church.)

Anyone with even a passing knowledge of the matter knows the issue is much broader than that. The town does own the clock, but the records clearly indicate that it does not own the rest of the building, and never did, including the steeple. The town has a mere right of way across the roof of the church to attend to its clock, and any suggestion that this fact alone requires contributing to a sprinkler system is pretty far out. The town should require the church to install a sprinkler in the steeple above the clock, and then the town could avoid any expenditure at all, just by relying on the trickle-down theory.

Furthermore, the limitless possibilities of separation of church and state are totally ignored in the article. In the past, opportunities of this sort would not be allowed to stagnate, but on the contrary would be used to fuel the argumentative fires and train orators for future Town Meetings, in keeping with the magnitude of the issue.

While all this was pretty discouraging, and exposed the flaccid persona of the present citizenry, the worst was yet to come. For many years we lived in what was an old woodworking shop on a lane behind the Town Hall. We rebuilt it over the years, and named it The Toy Shop. Next to it was an old barn in which we parked our cars. Just across the lane from the barn was an embankment that formed the hind end of the cemetery and served to keep everyone inside. Set in the embankment was a lone tablet, set in a granite wall. The old slate tablet contained one name, "The Hon. Sam L. Dana," and the date, 1794.

In the course of my various doings as Town Counsel years ago, I discovered that The Hon. Sam L. Dana had been a forceful figure in town, both feared and revered by everyone, not the least of all by his own family. Toward the end of his life, he apparently was in a down period family-wise, and on his deathbed threatened to return and haunt those left behind if they as much as thought about planting him in the family plot with the rest of his relatives. Believing him capable of doing so, his survivors elected to slide him feet first into the embankment behind the cemetery. They plugged the entrance with granite blocks and attached the slate plaque to commemorate the event.

In the course of clearing brush and brambles from the embankment in my ongoing efforts to make something of the place, I exposed the wall and plaque. It was in poor repair, so I pointed up the stonework, cleaned up the plaque, and regularly thereafter attended to its maintenance. This was not a labor of love, but rather to make sure Sam L. did not slide out or suffer the ravages woodchucks cause to such sites once they begin to deteriorate. Anyway, if the tales about him were even half true, he was a genuine character, the likes of which no longer exist. He deserved preservation for that reason alone.

Though I had left his final resting place in good shape when we moved away, those who succeeded us in The Toy Shop took no such pains. The site has begun to deteriorate again. Gone are the mossy granite stones, gone is the old slate plaque with the name and date.

As I stood gazing at this desecration, I sensed a hand on my shoulder, and heard a voice that seemed to come from everywhere.

"Don't worry, boy," it said, "you done right by me. Them's that say there ain't no tomorrow will live to regret it, believe me."

And I do believe him.